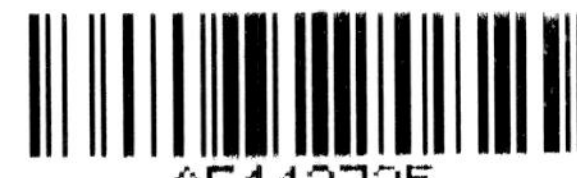
AF442725

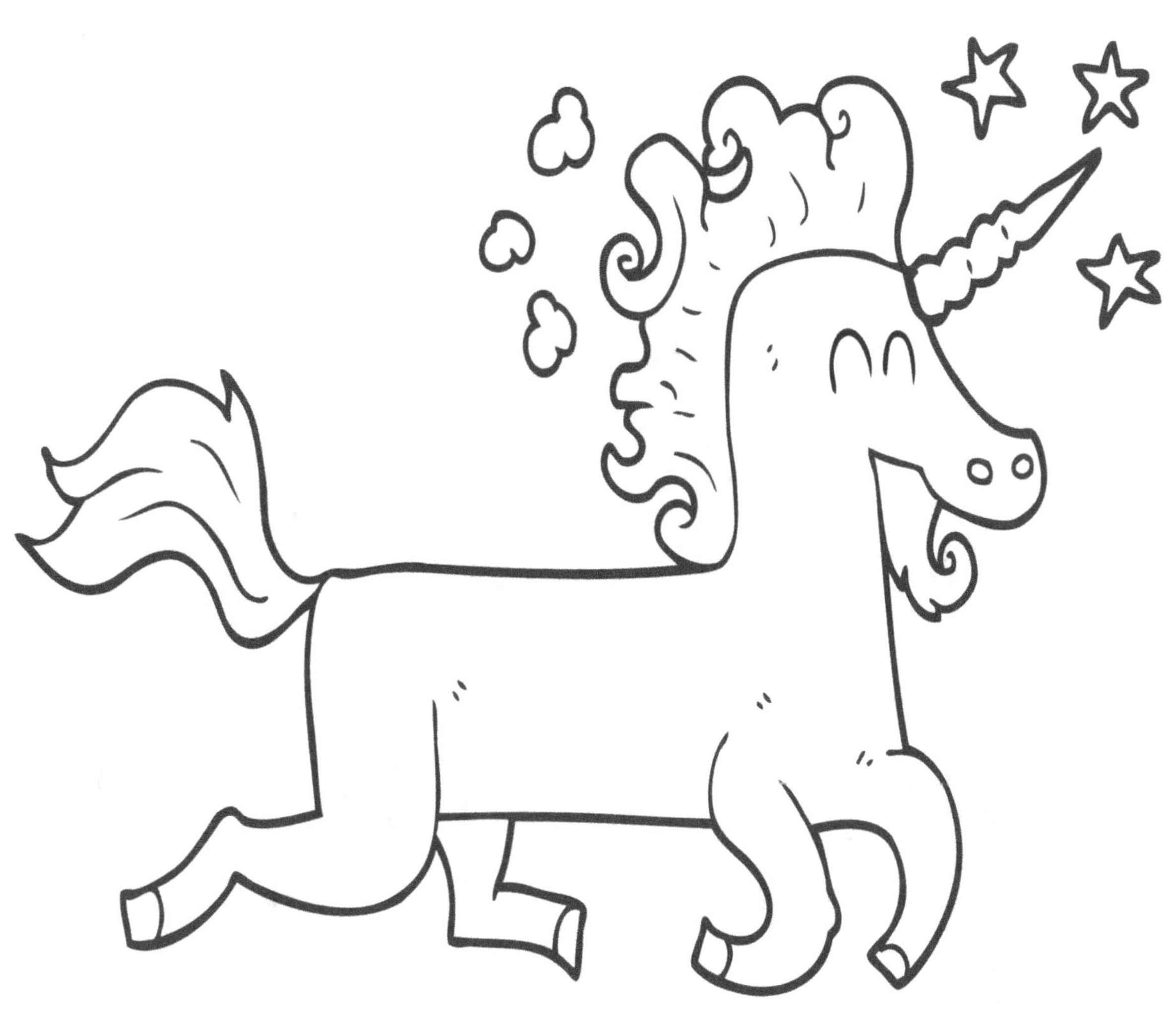

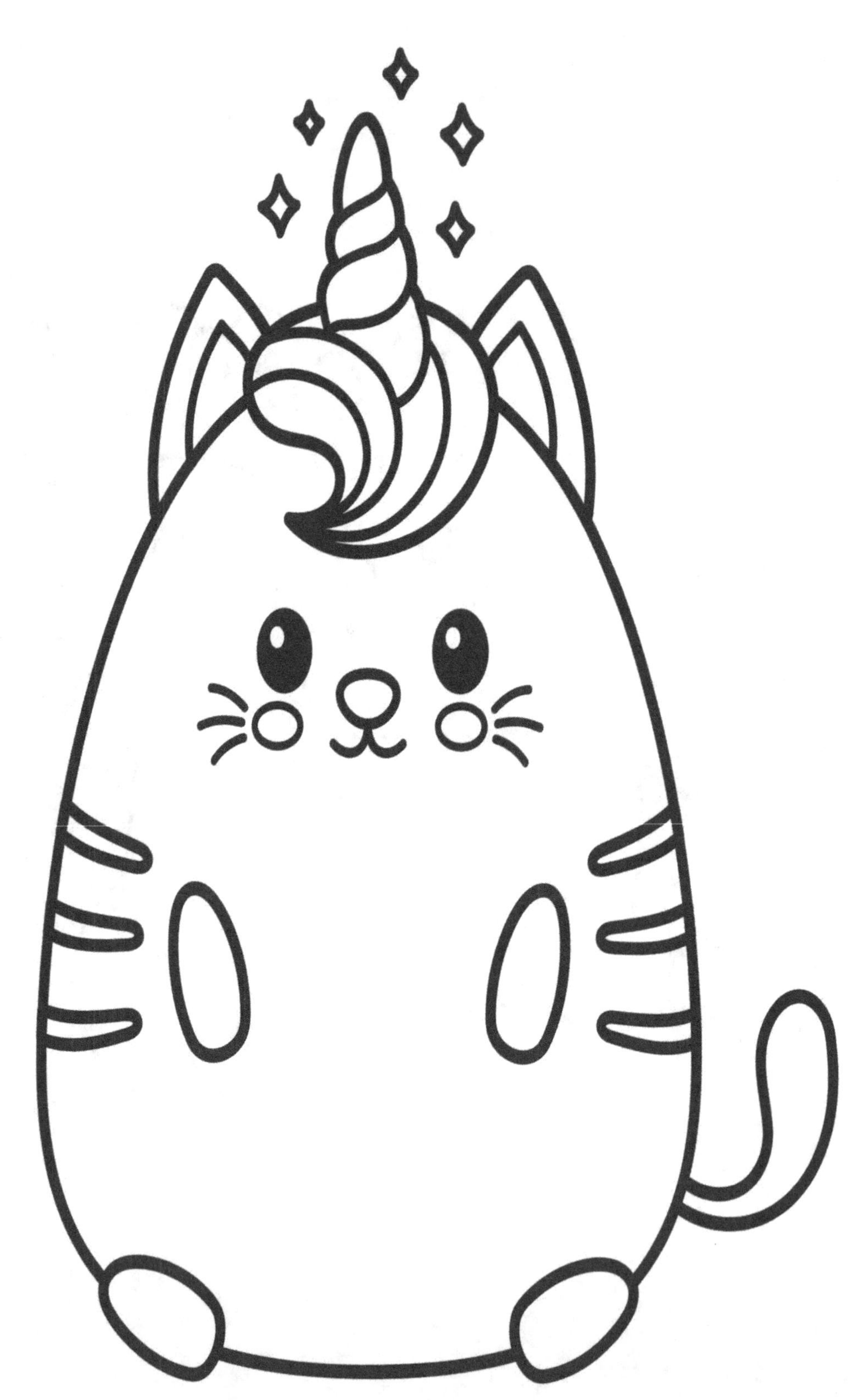

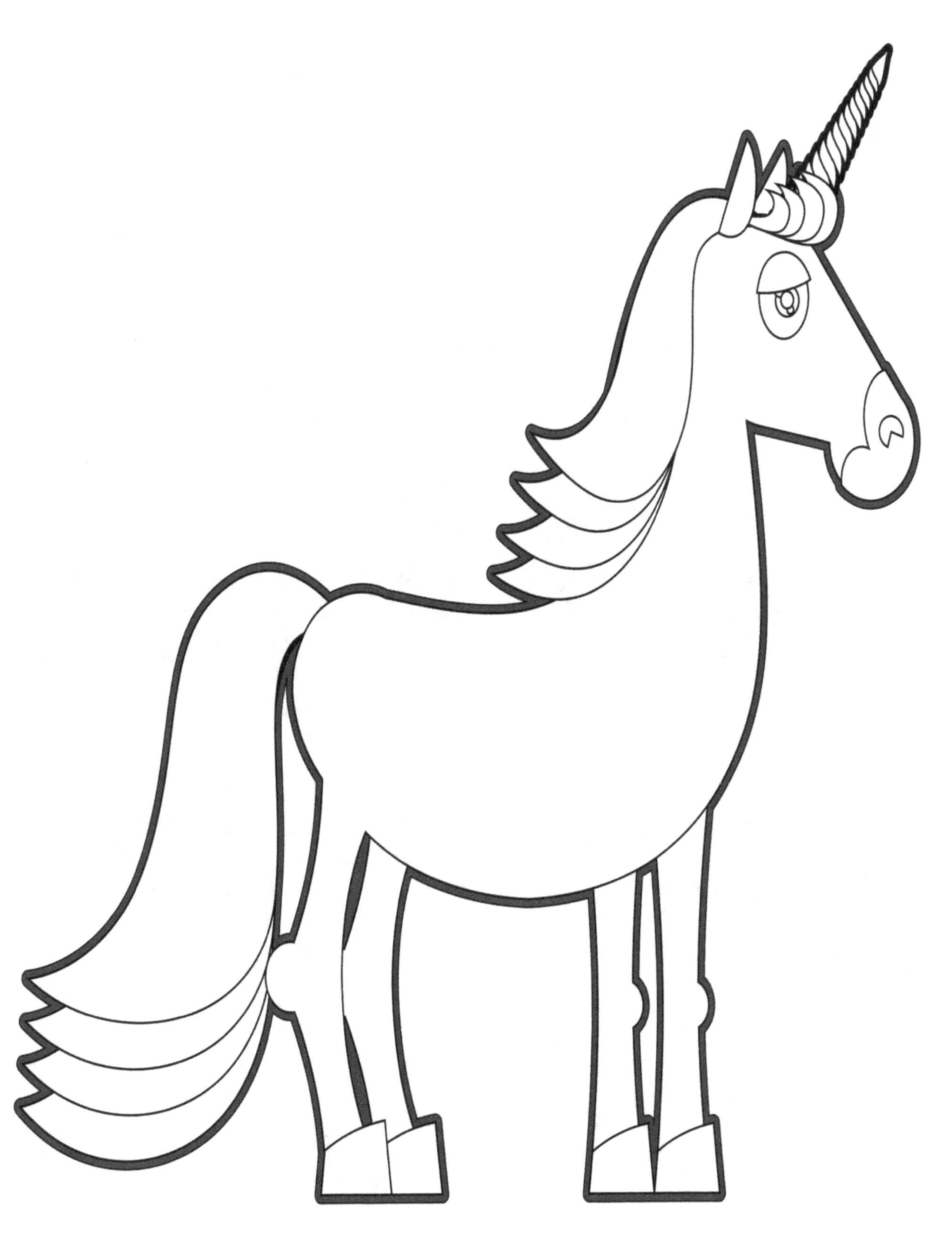

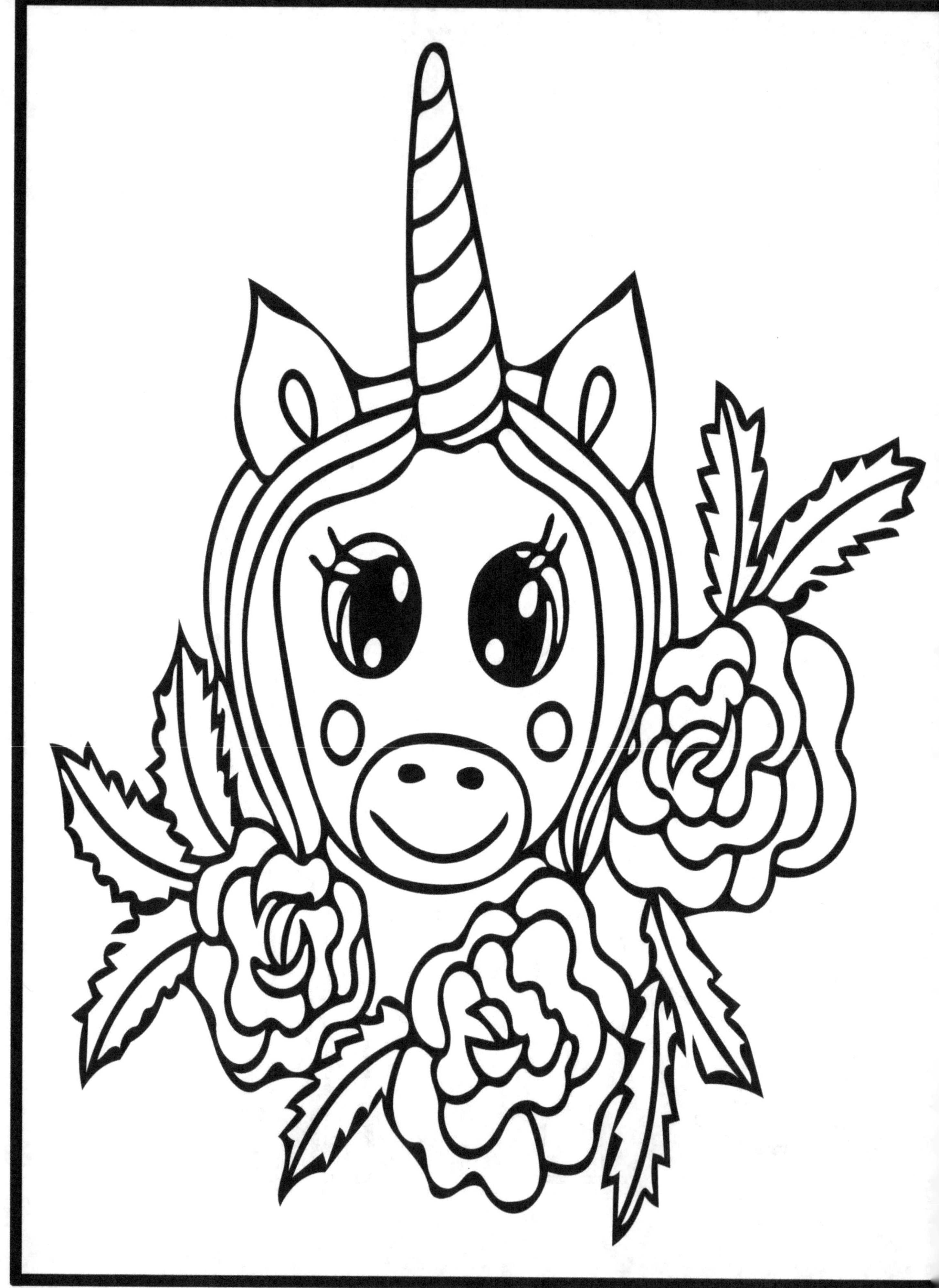

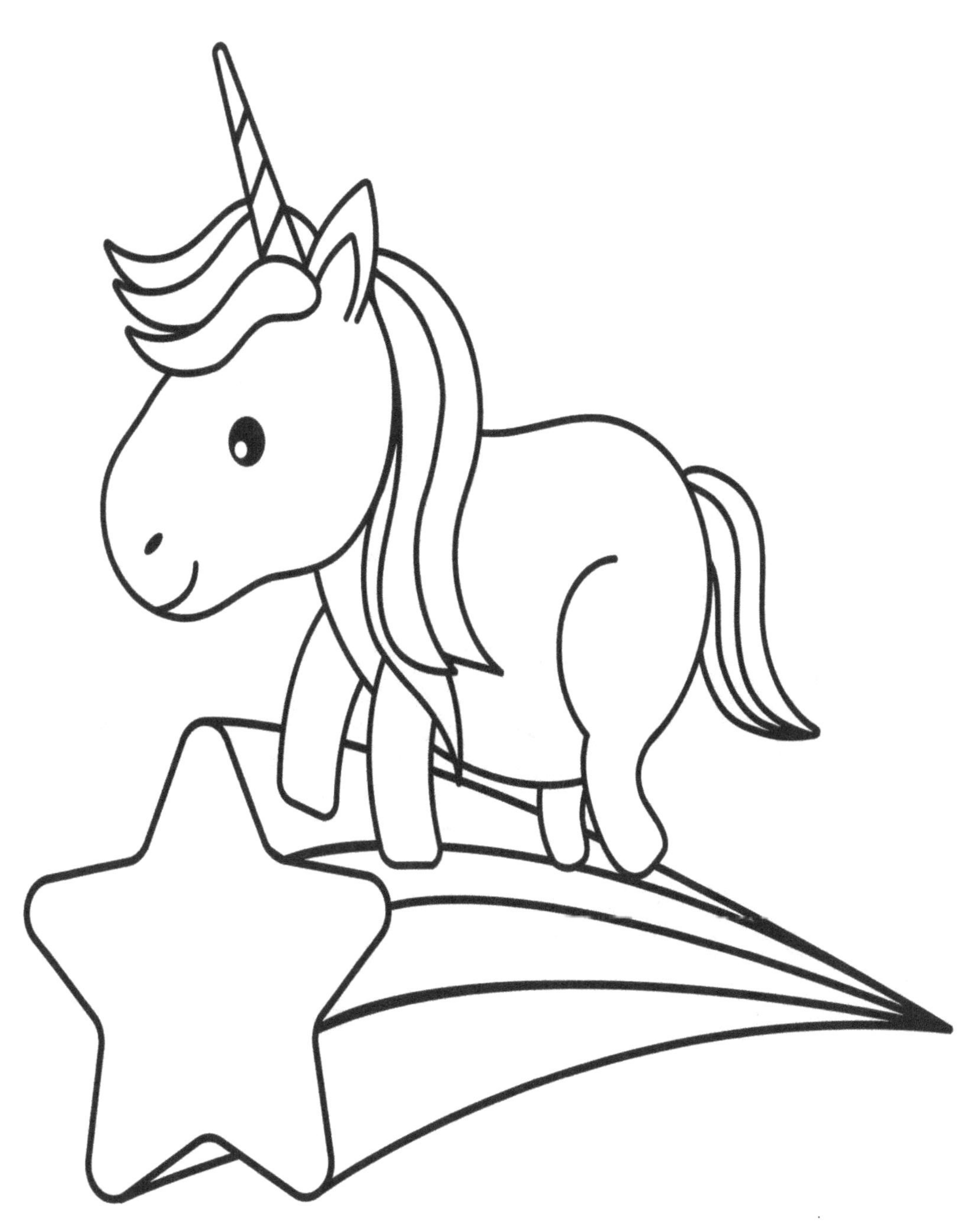

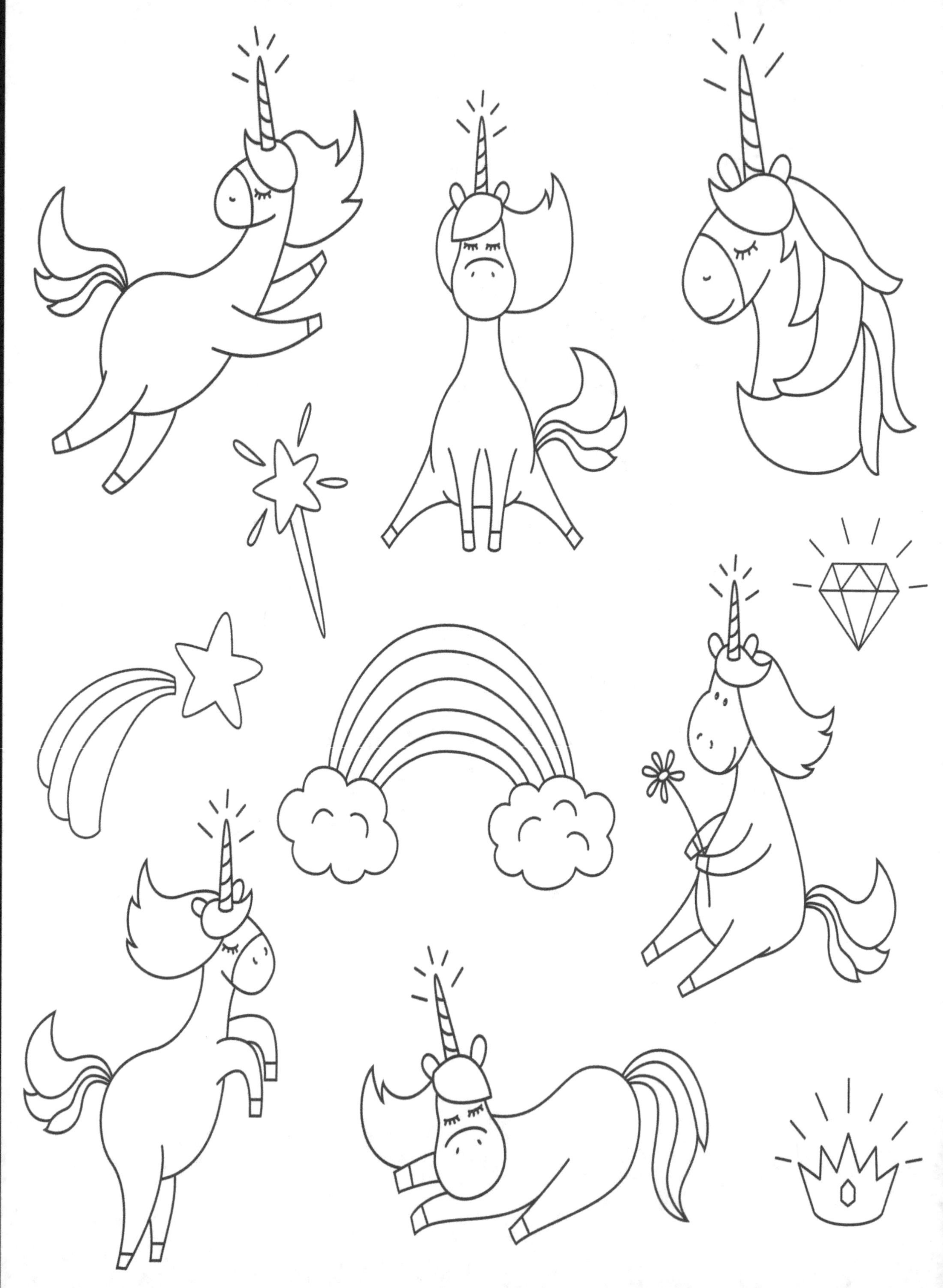

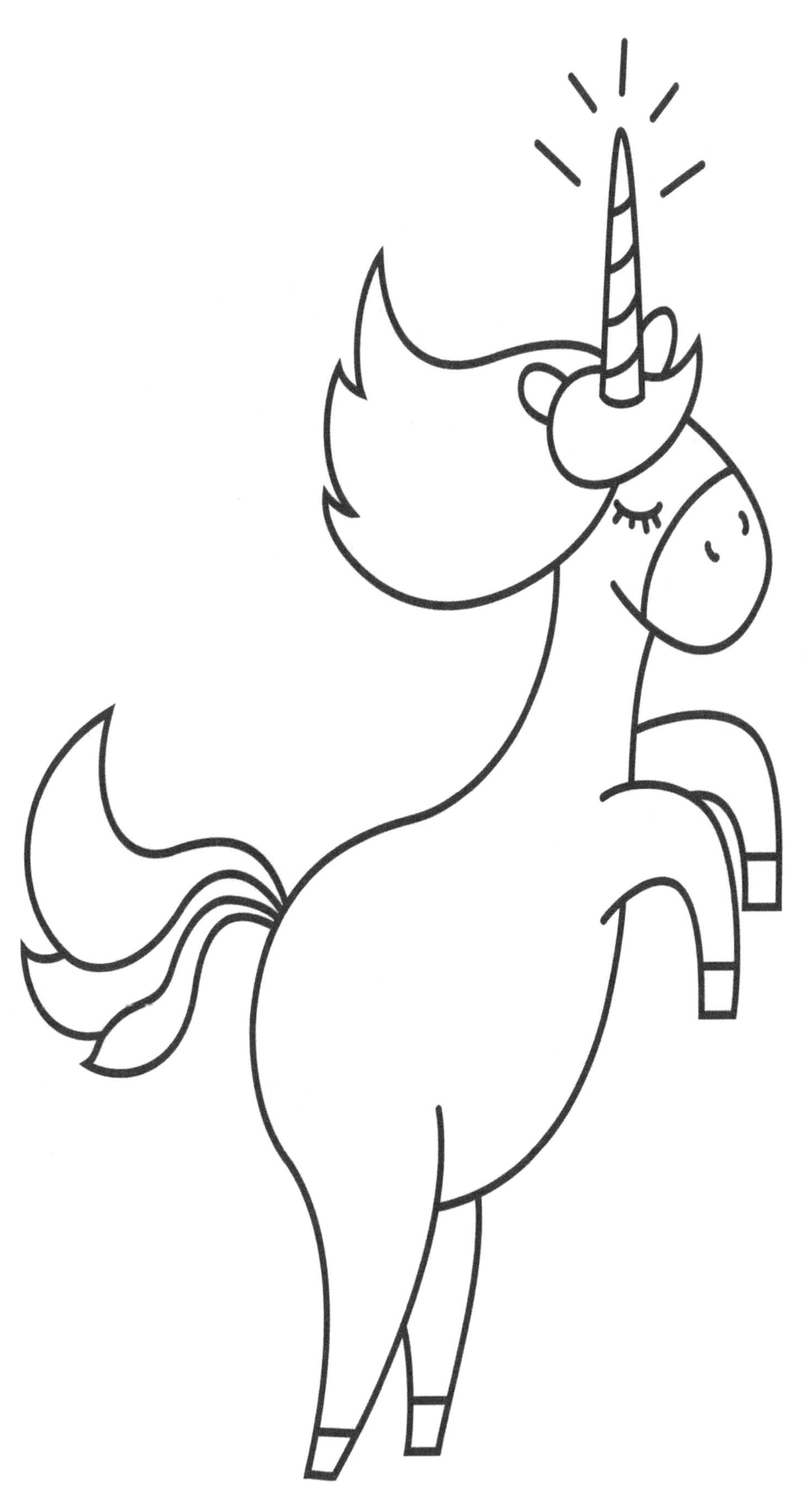

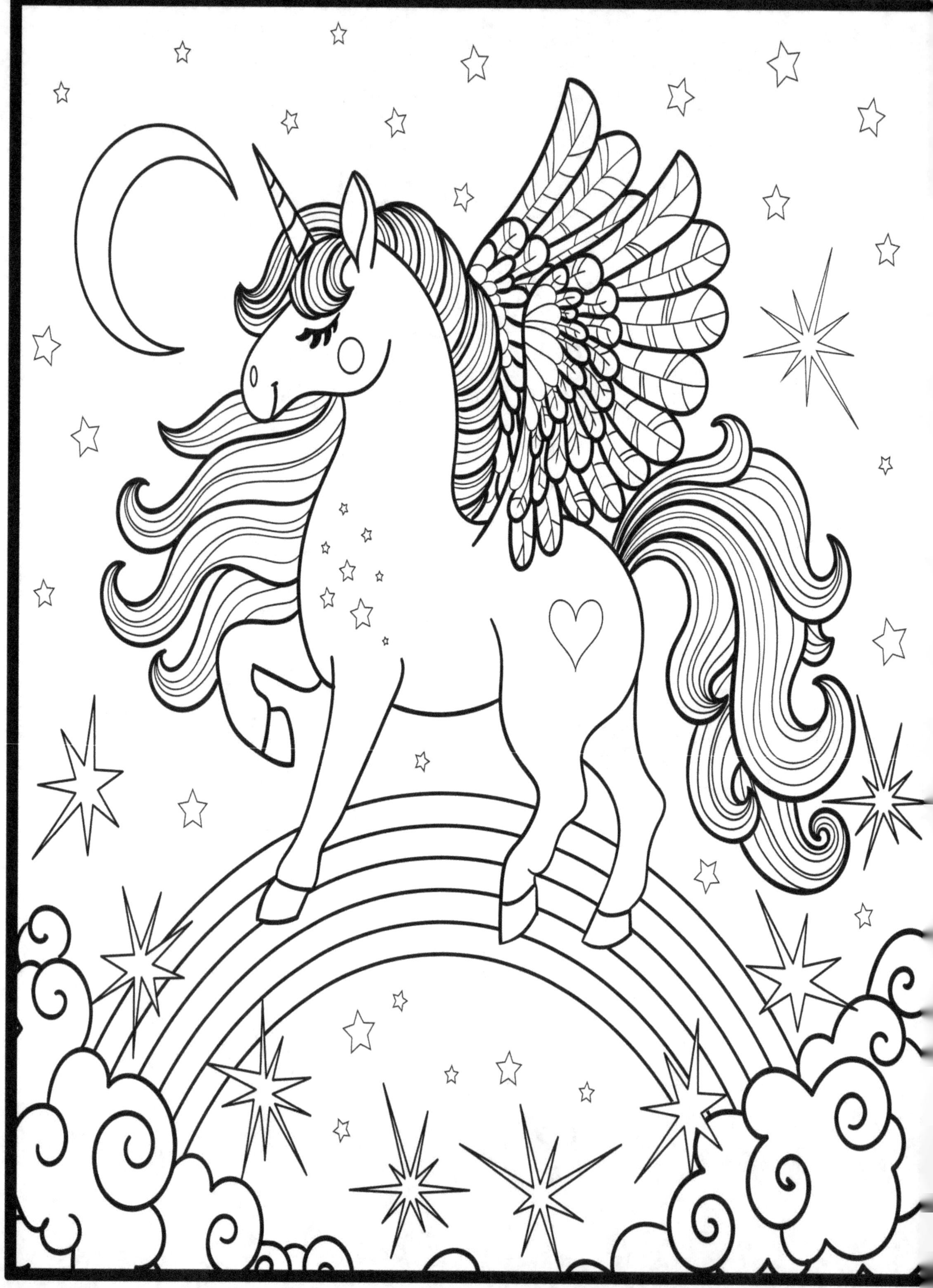

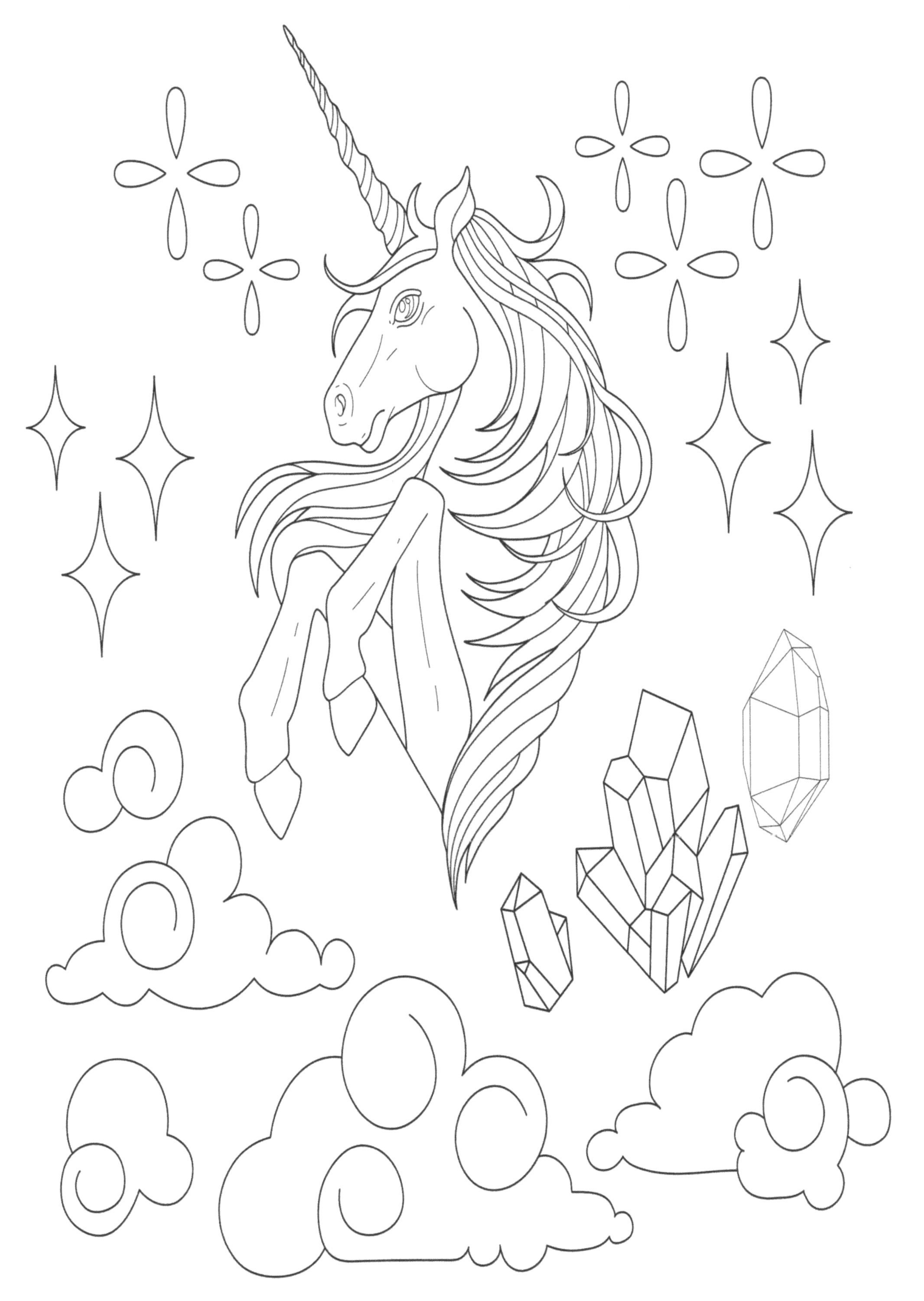

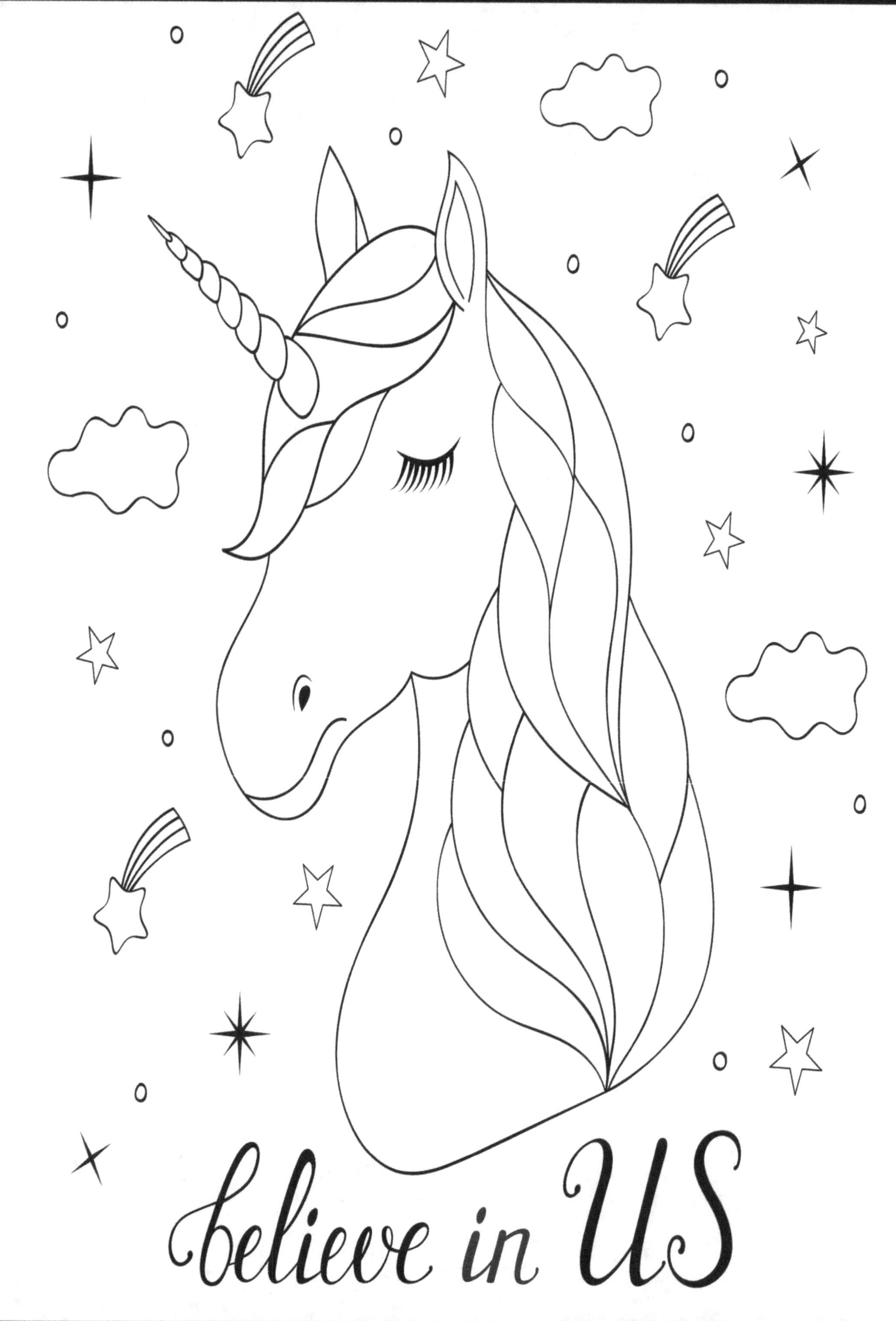

believe in US

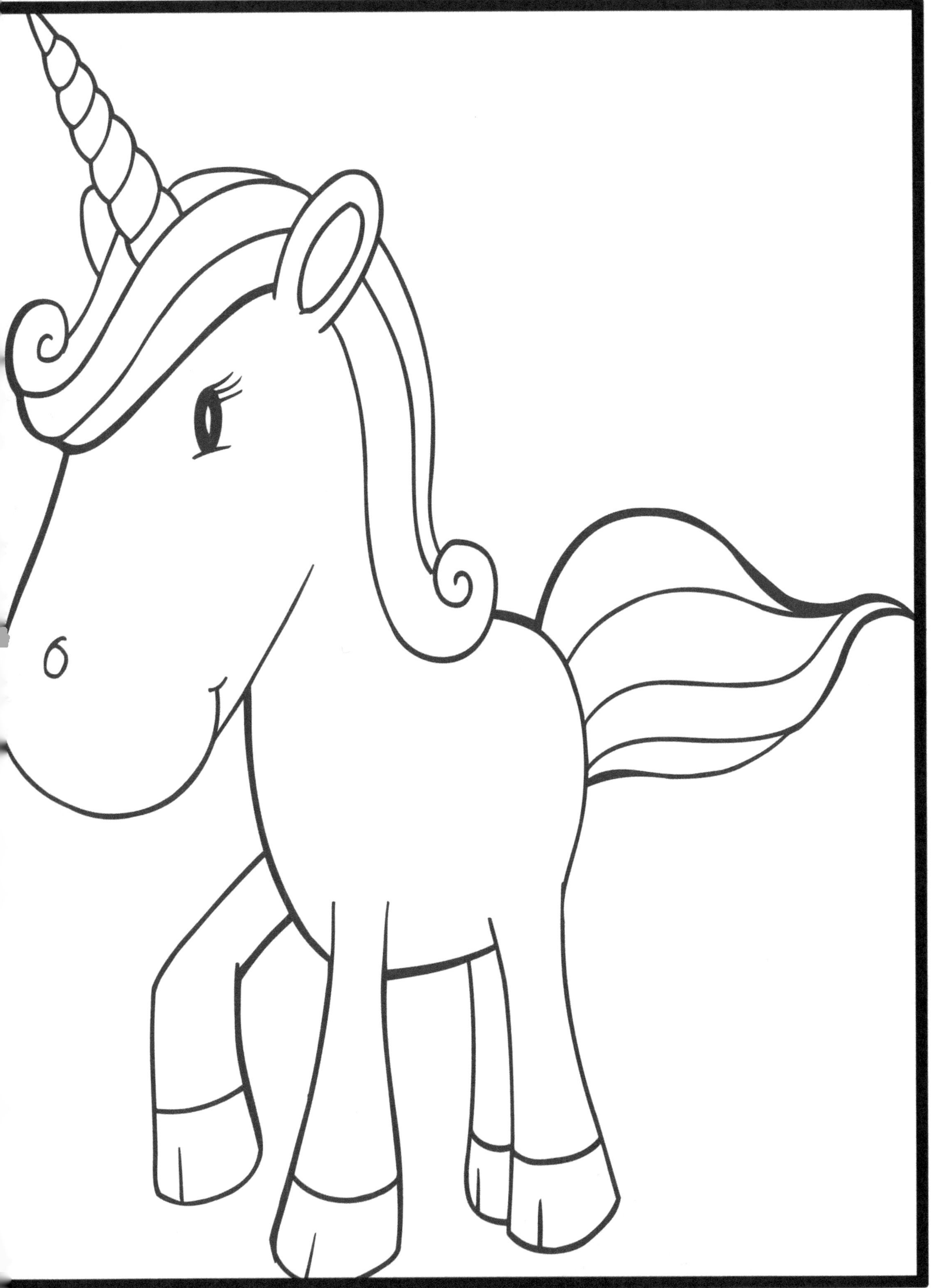

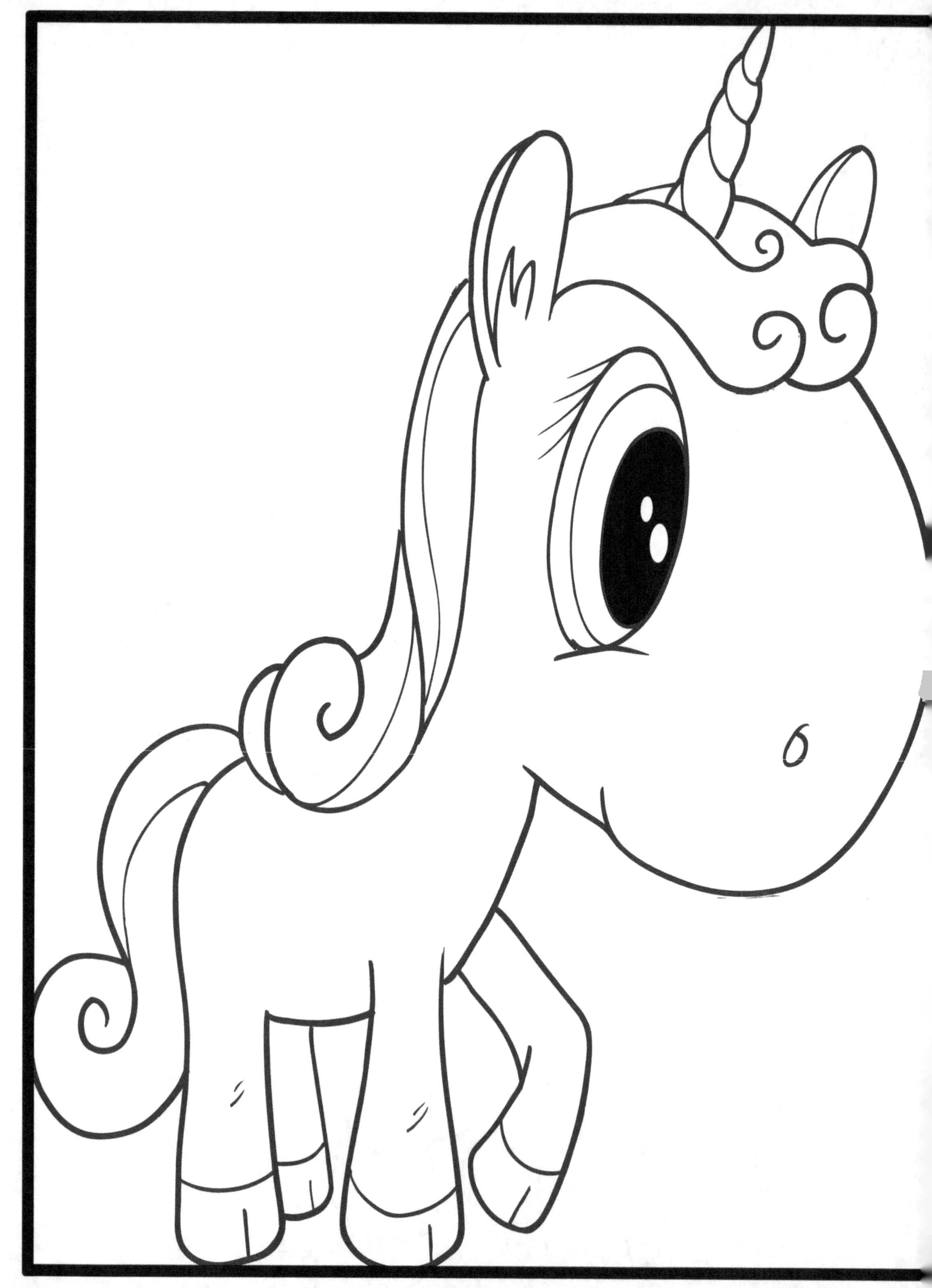

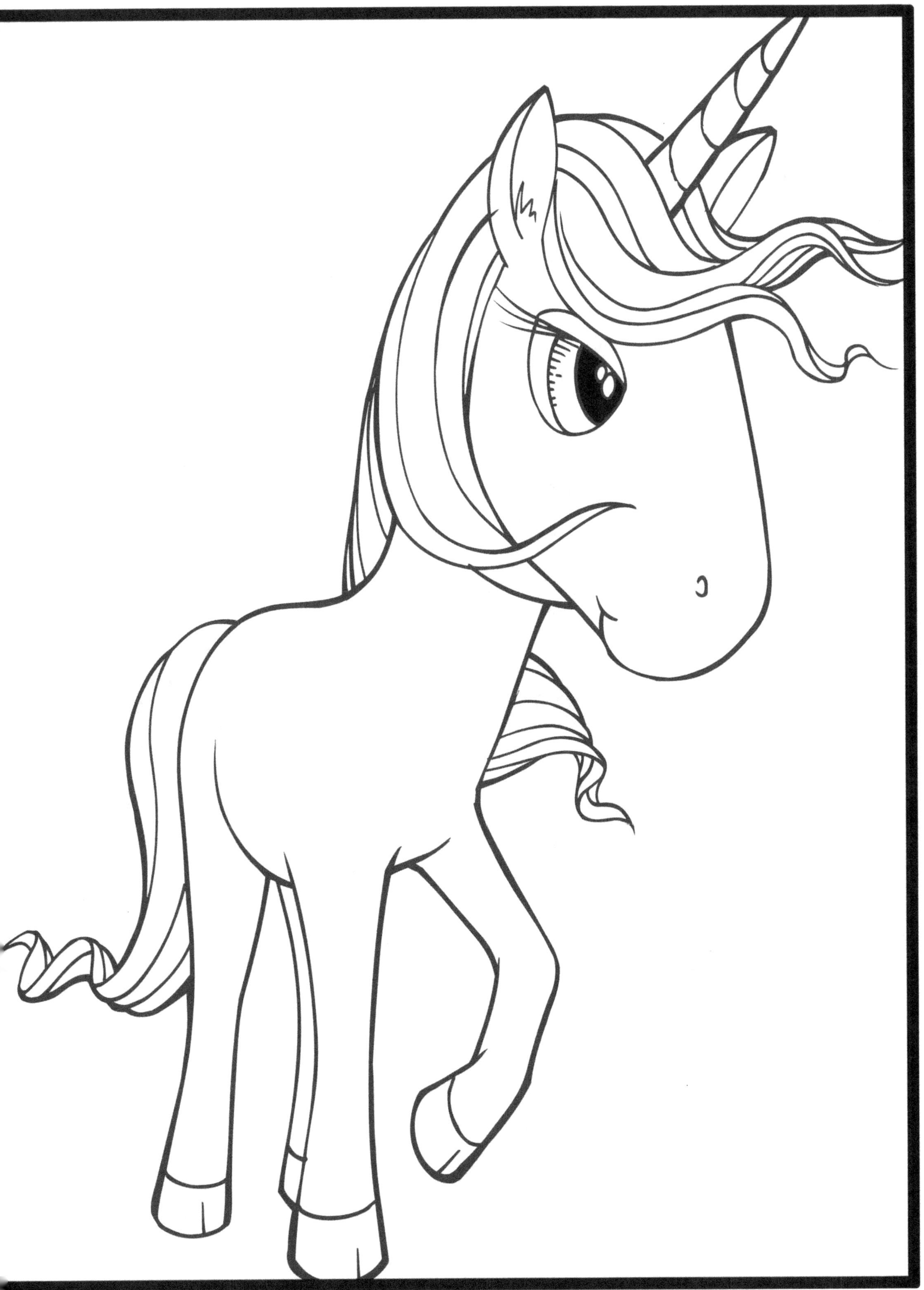

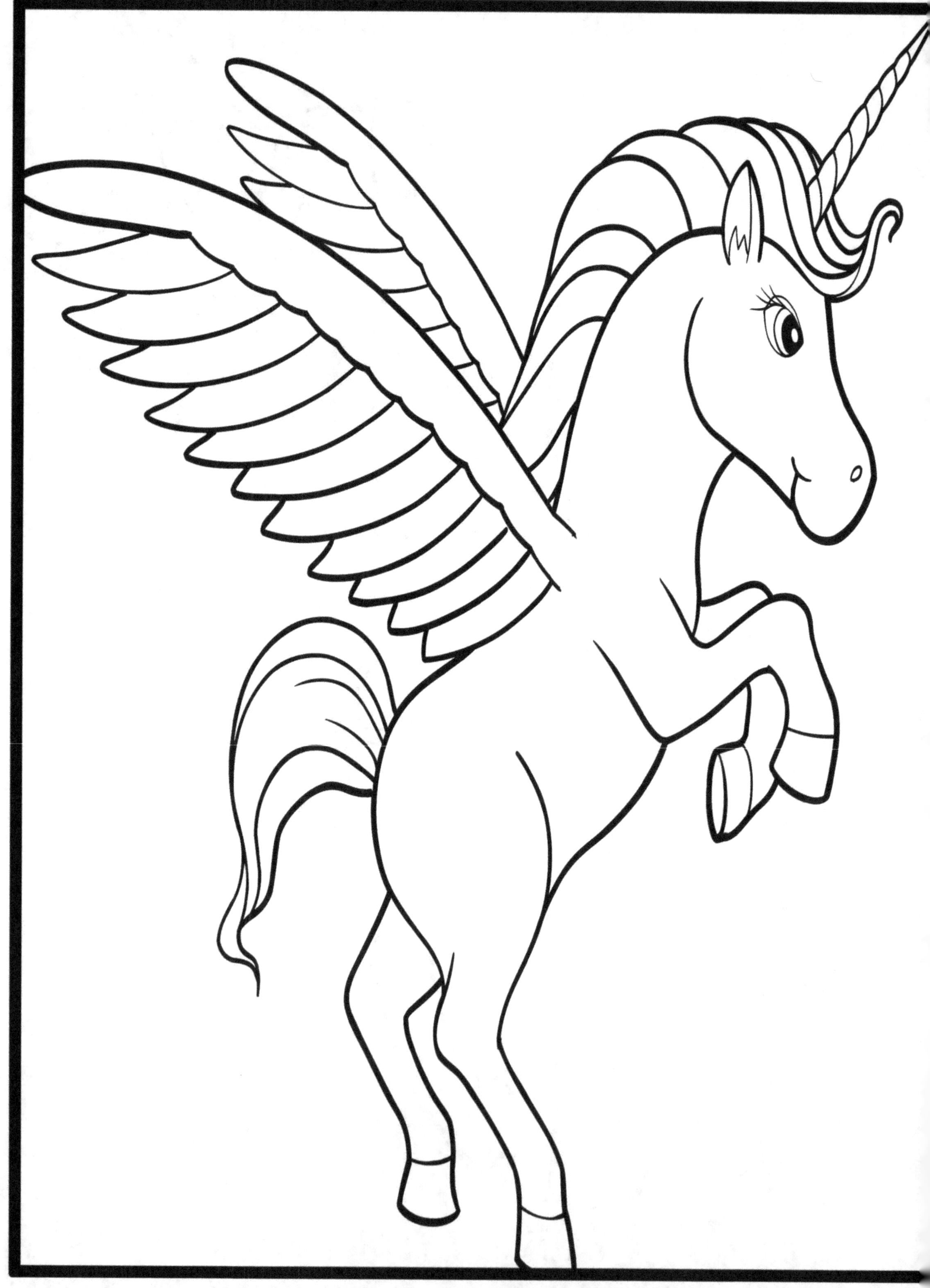

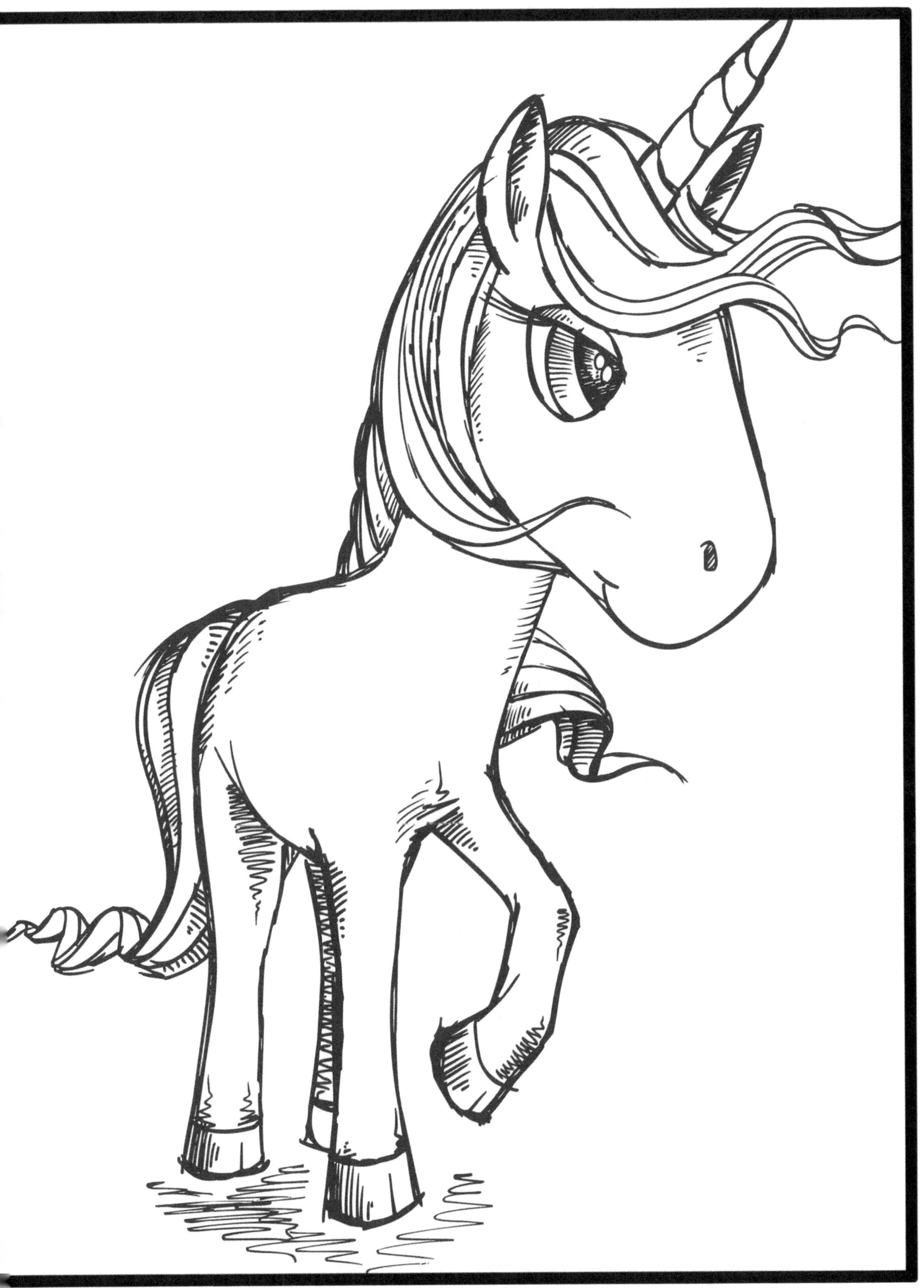

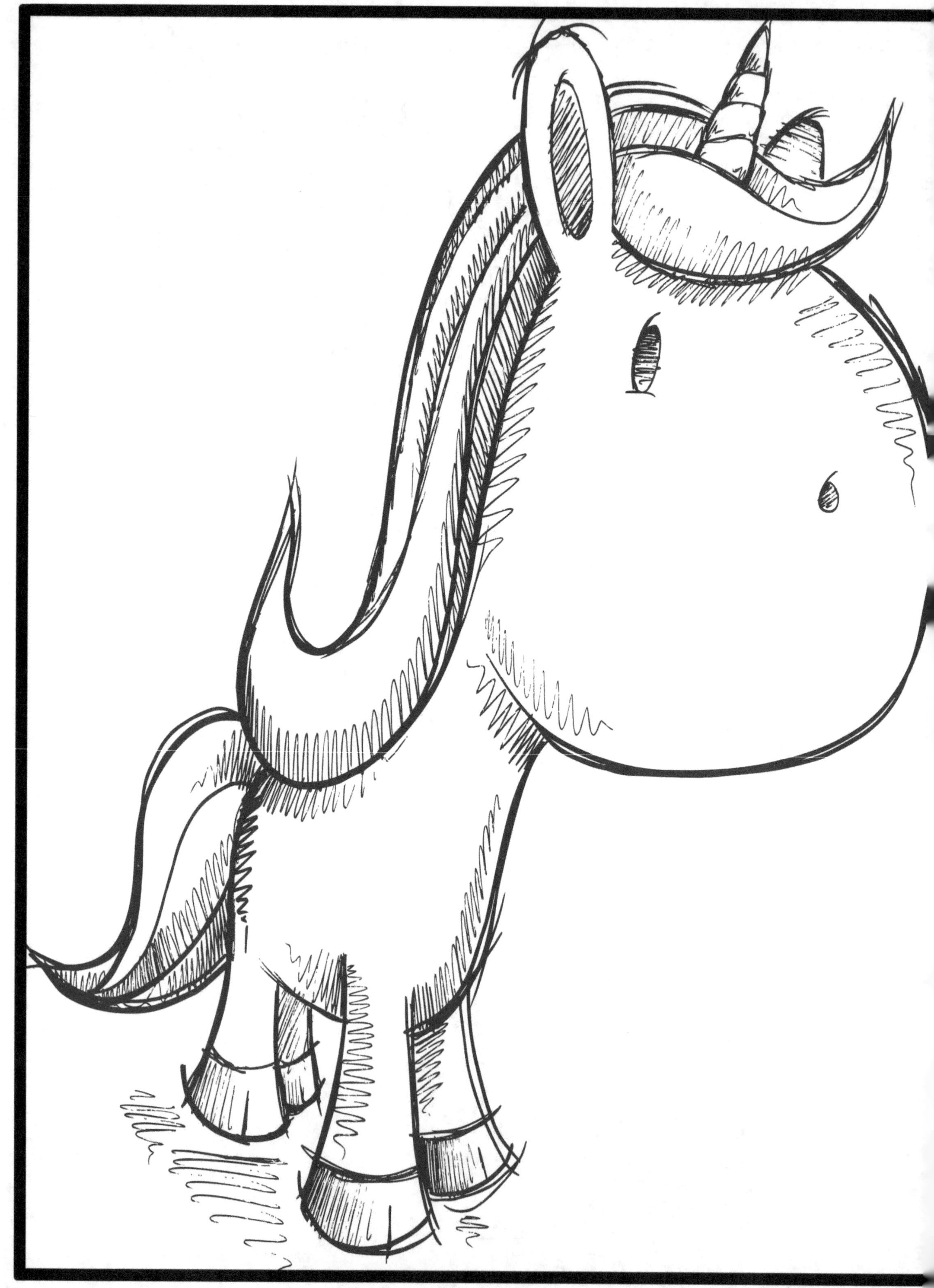

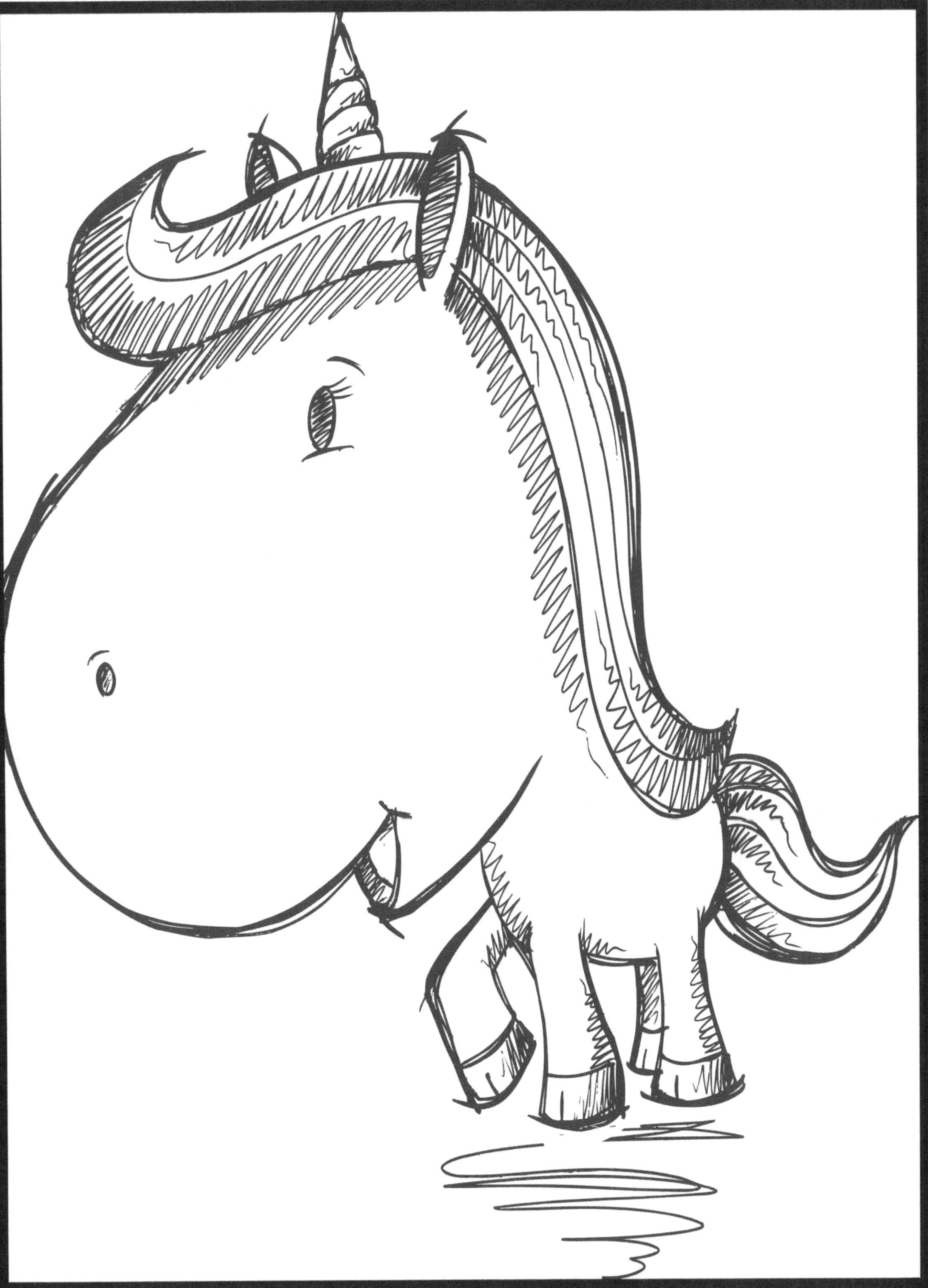

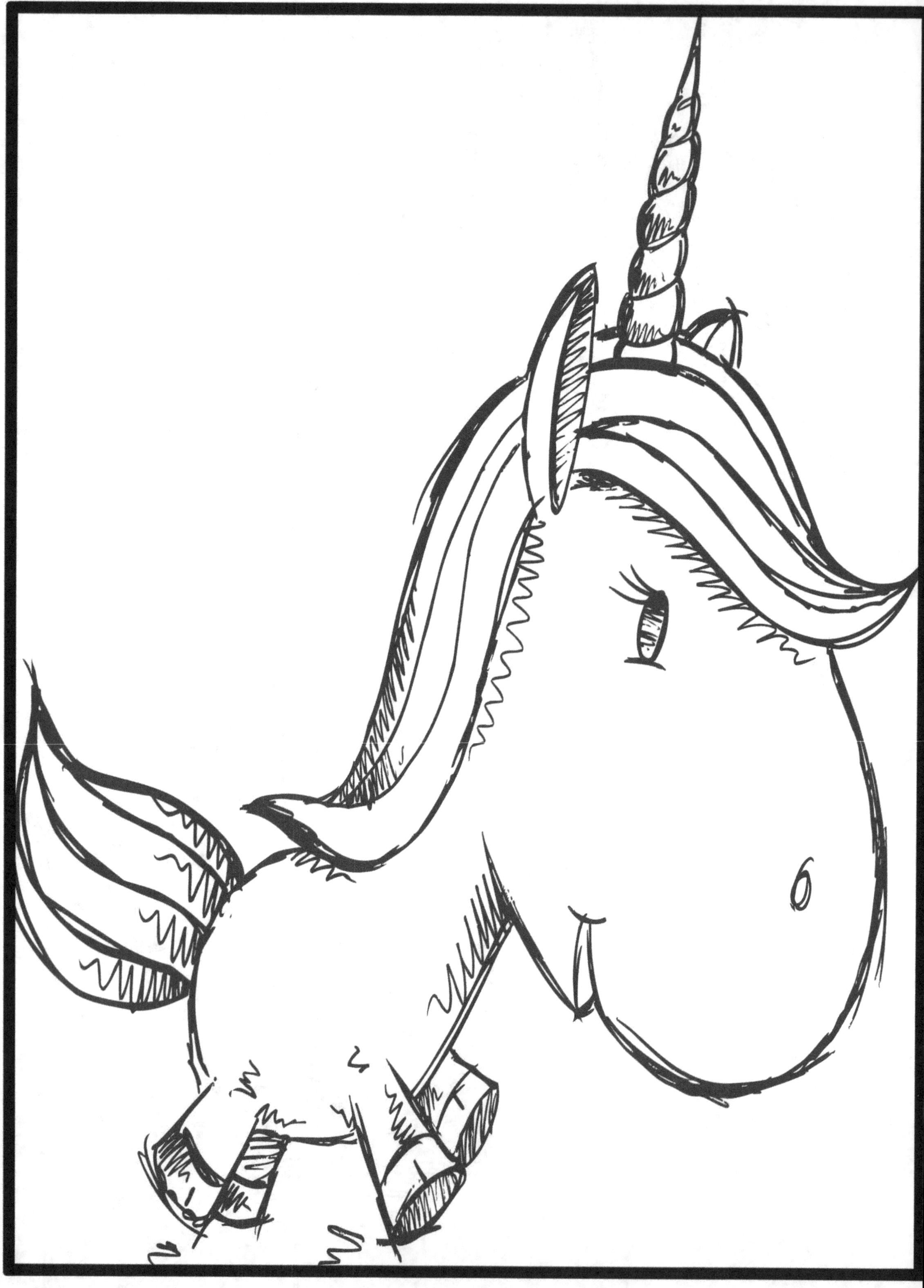

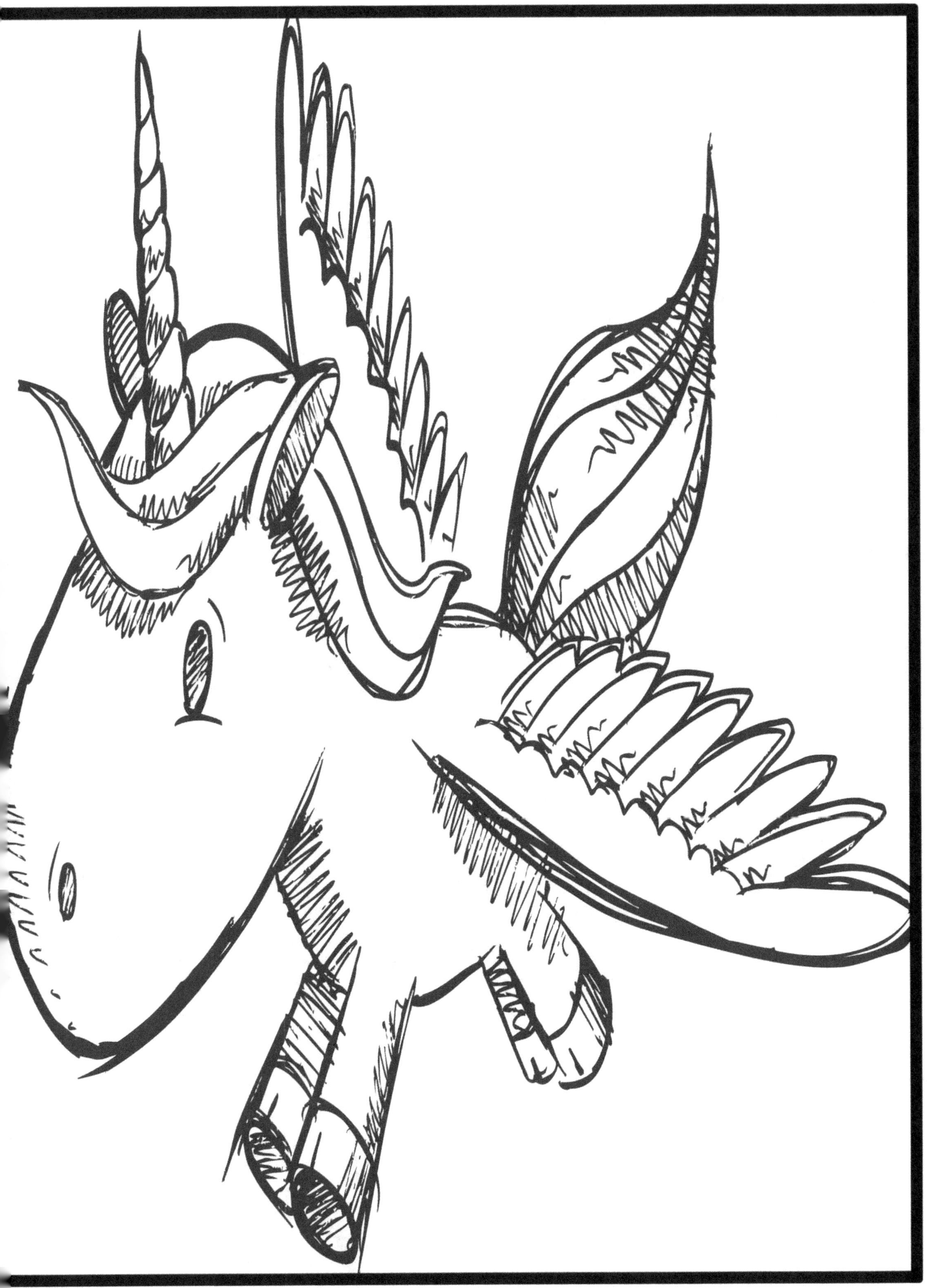

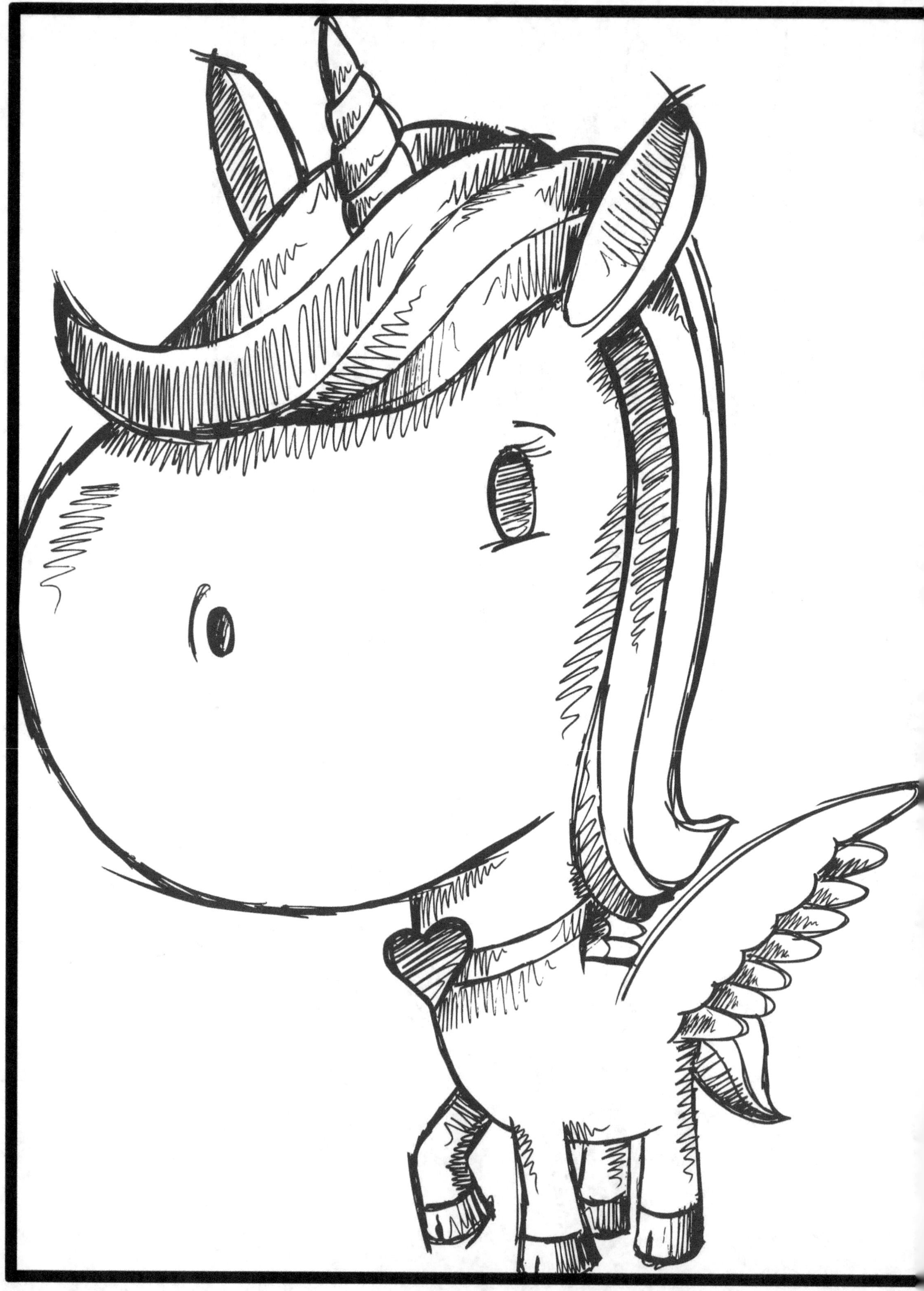

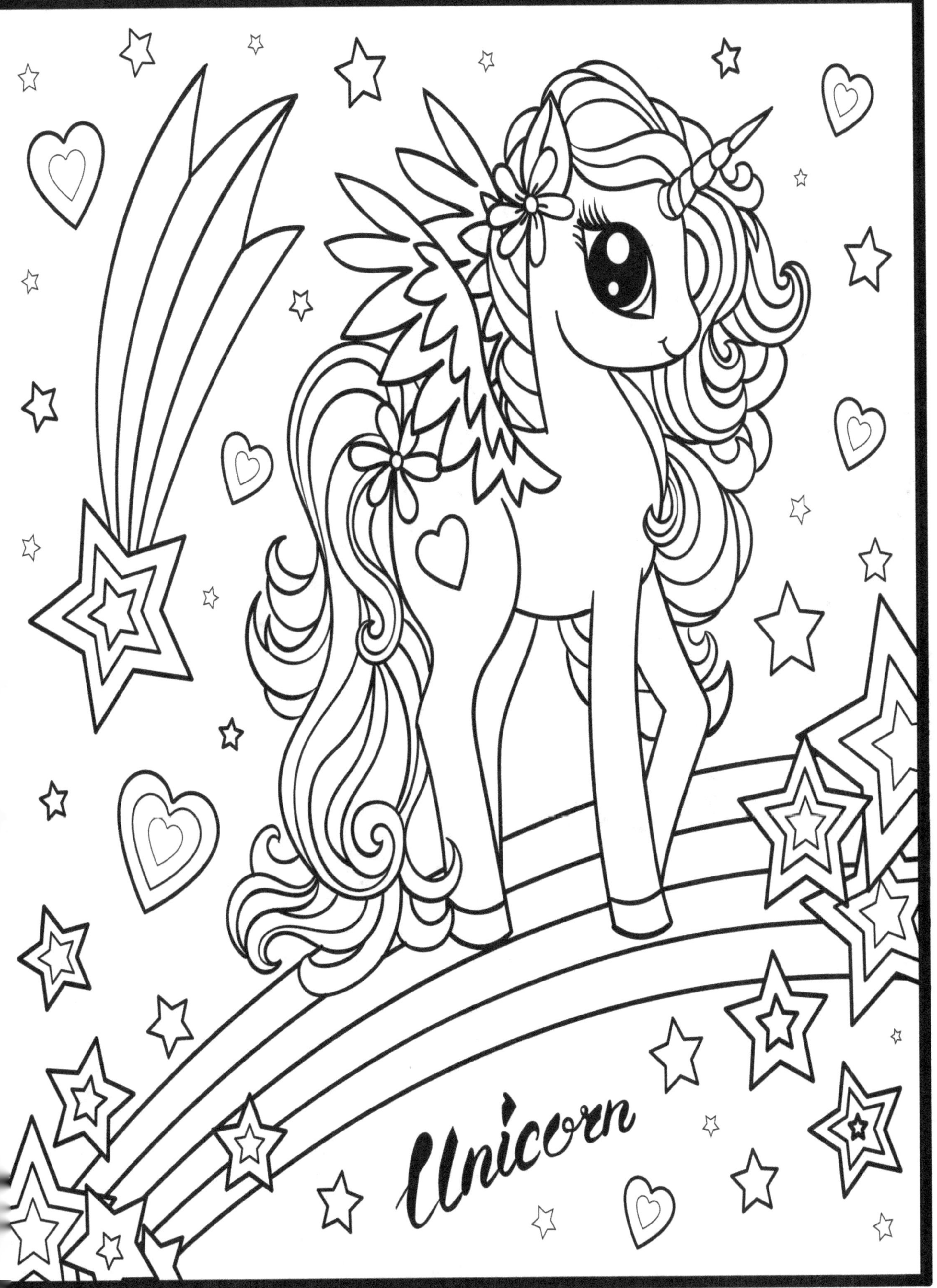
Unicorn

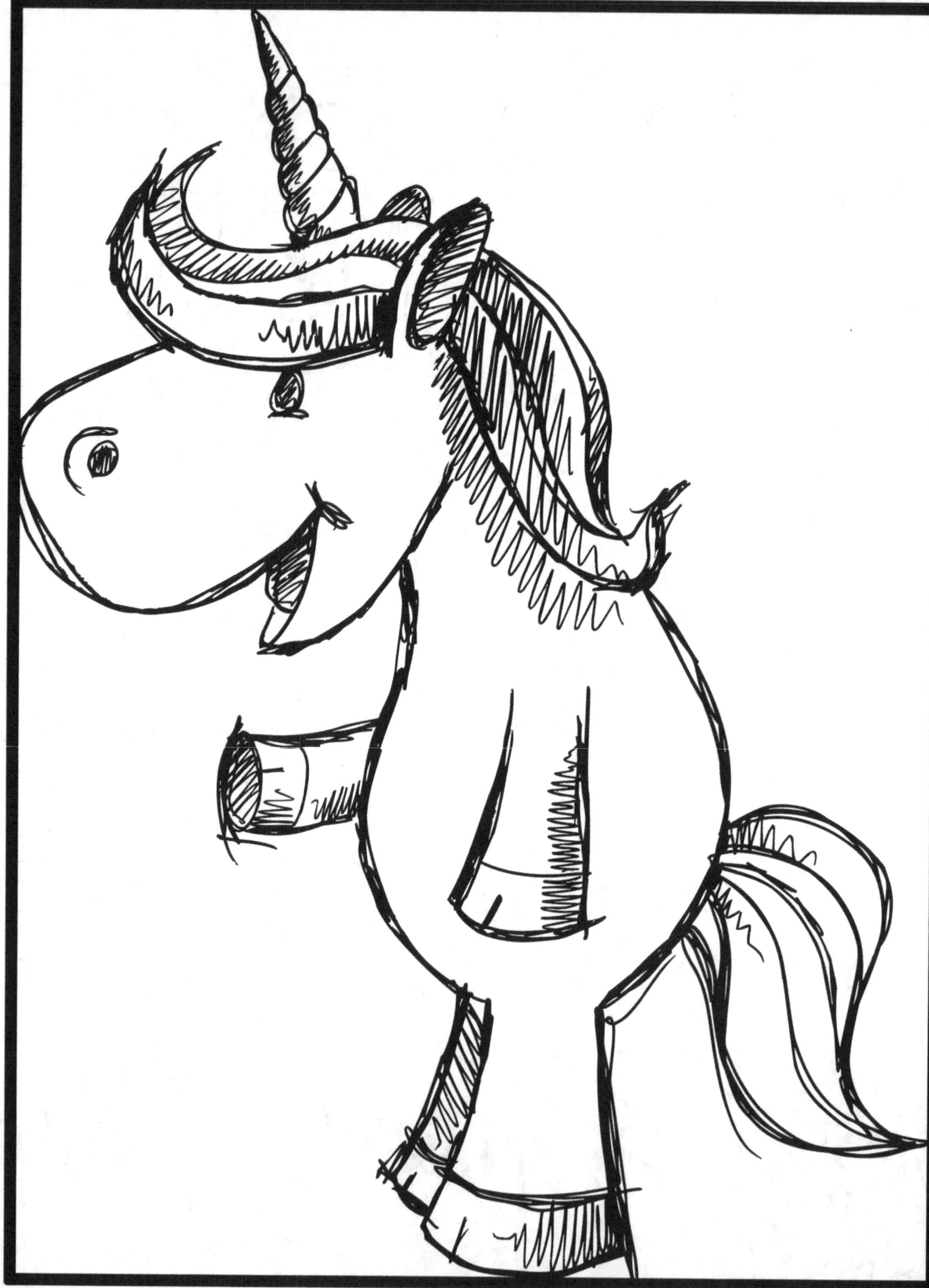

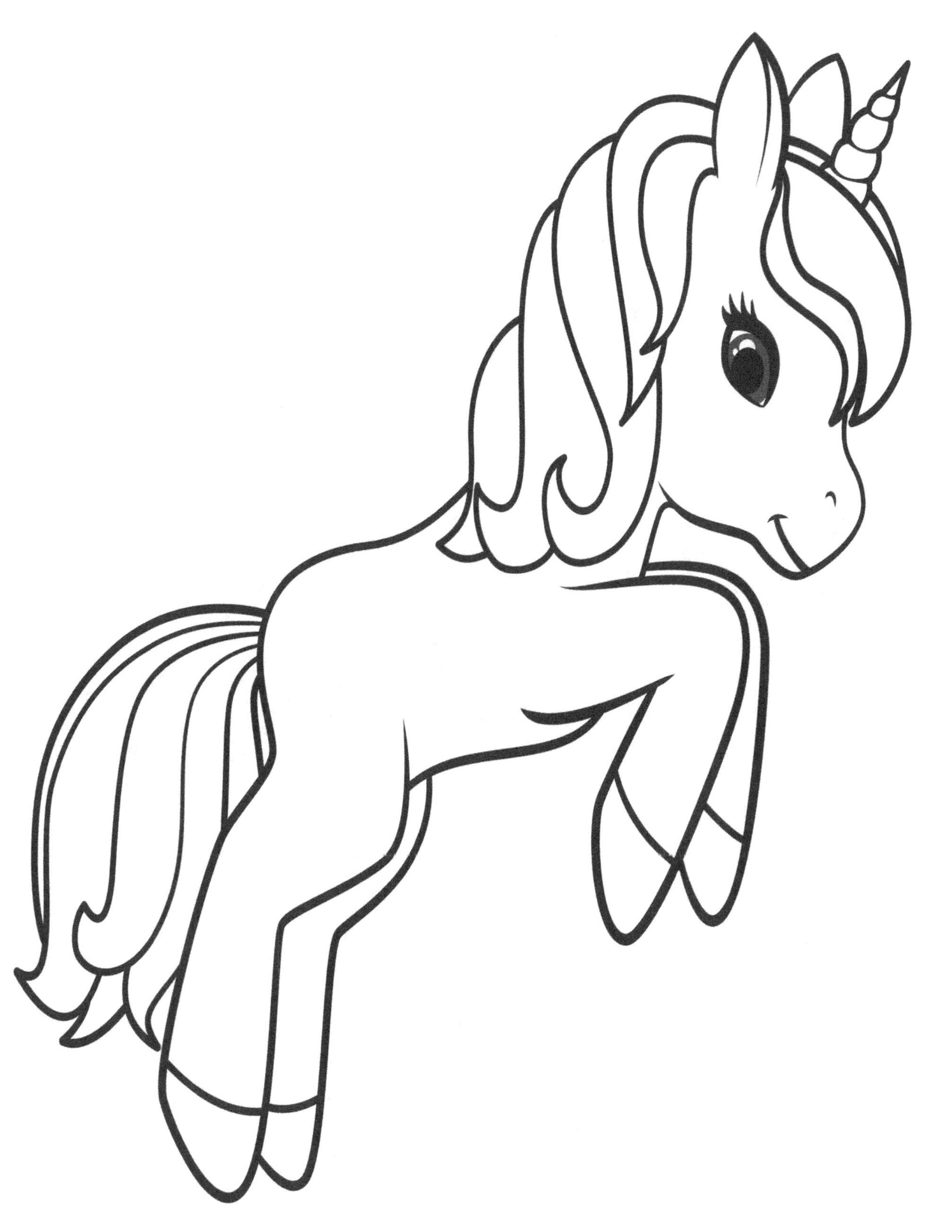

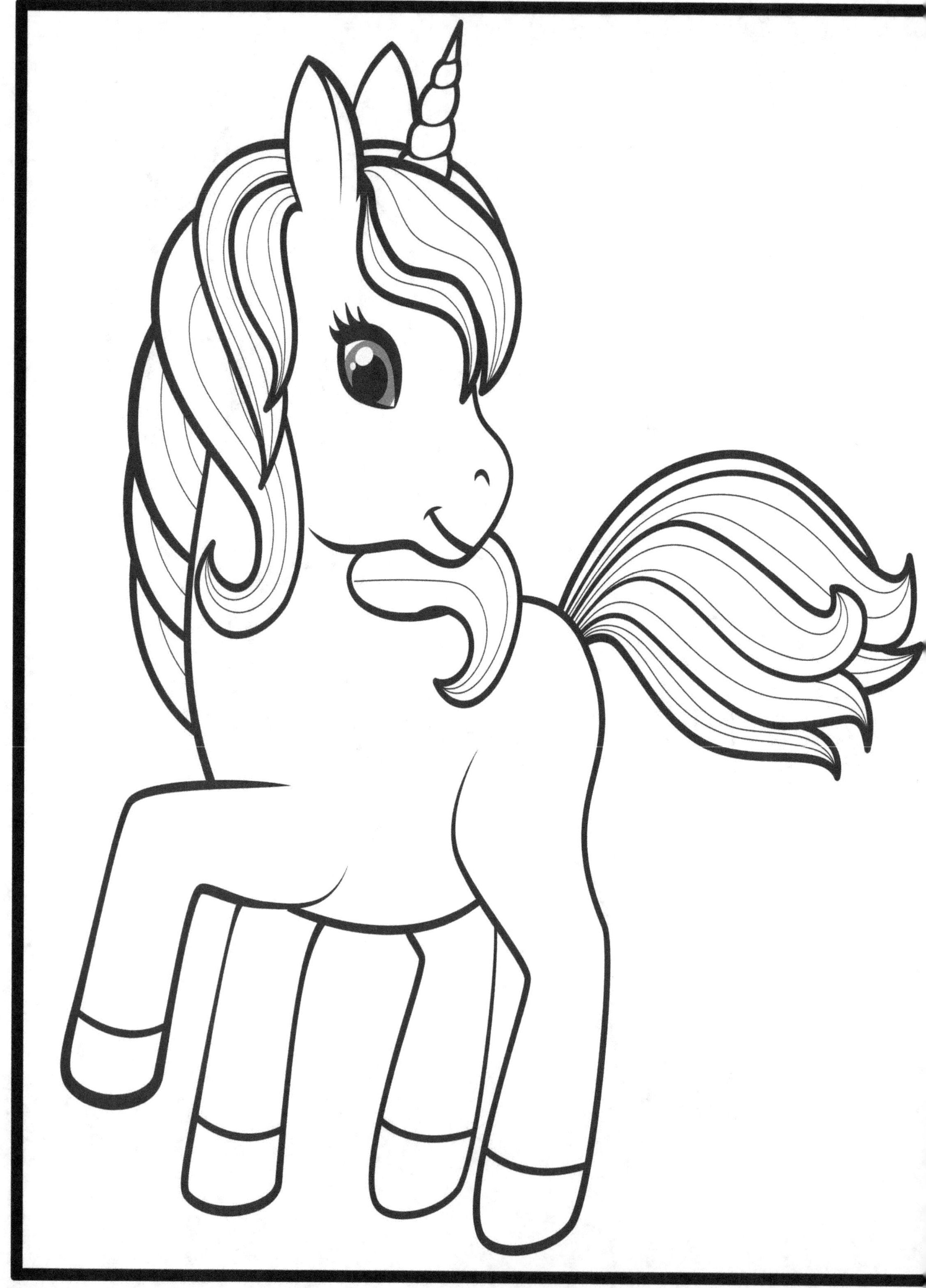

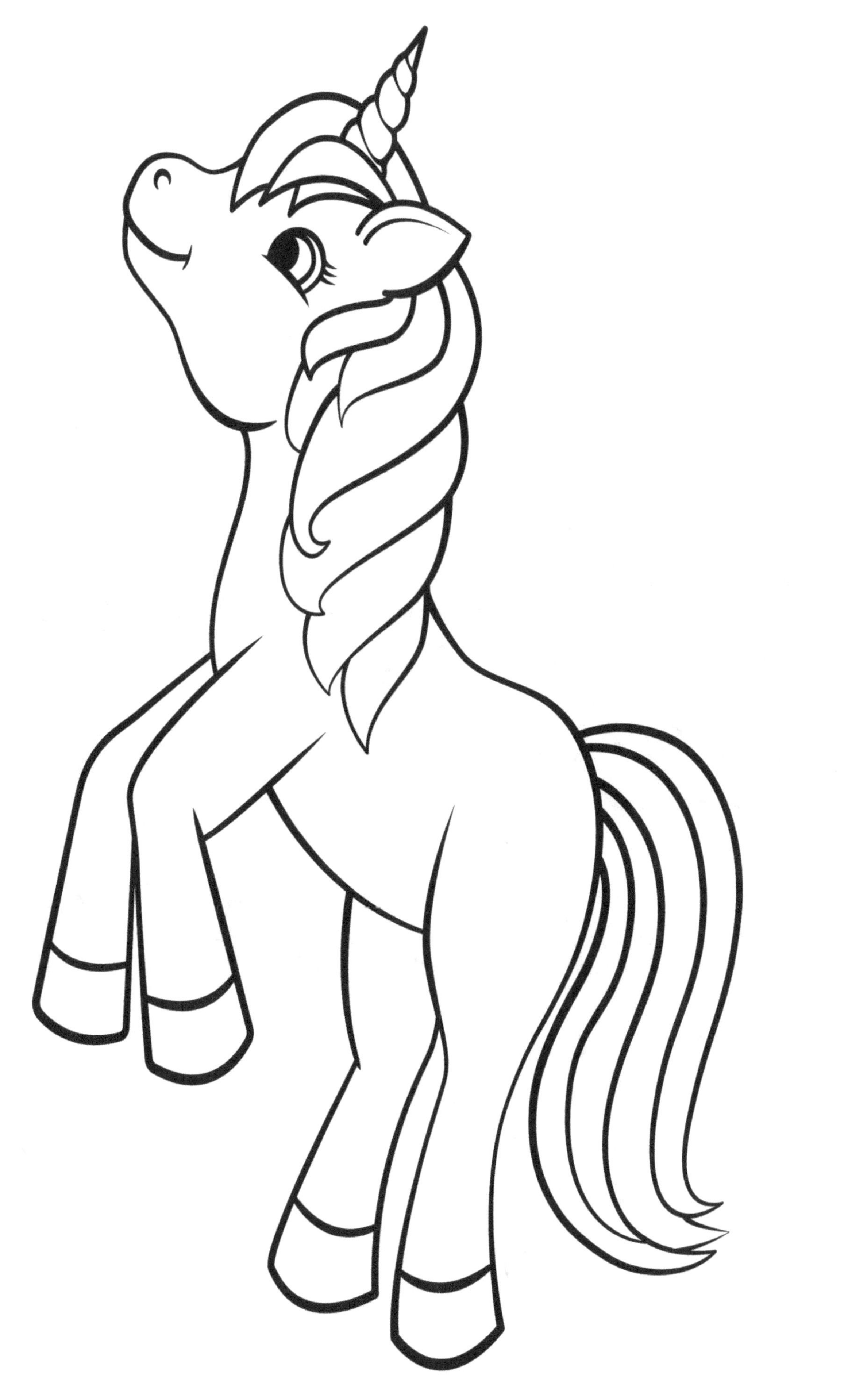

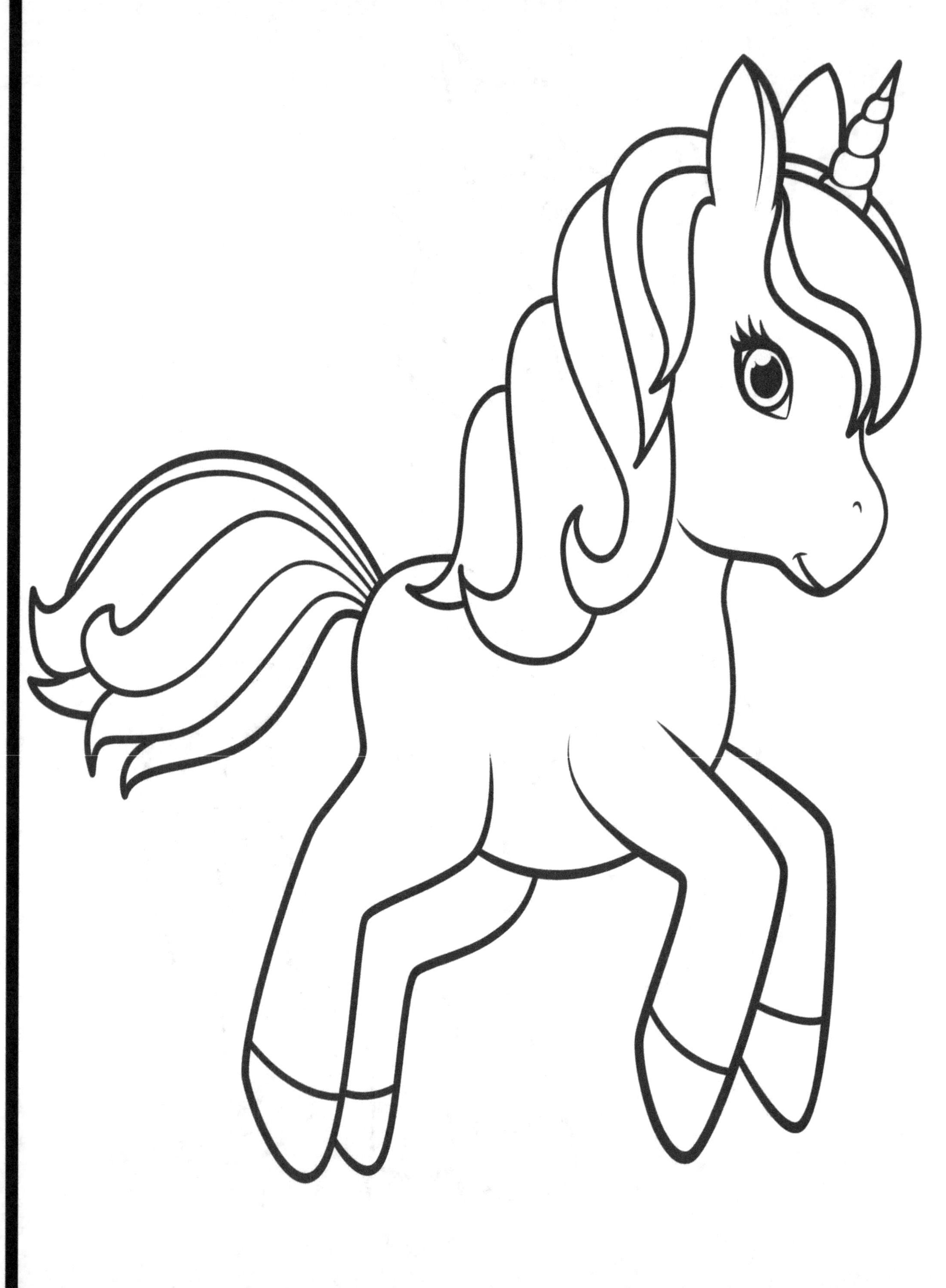

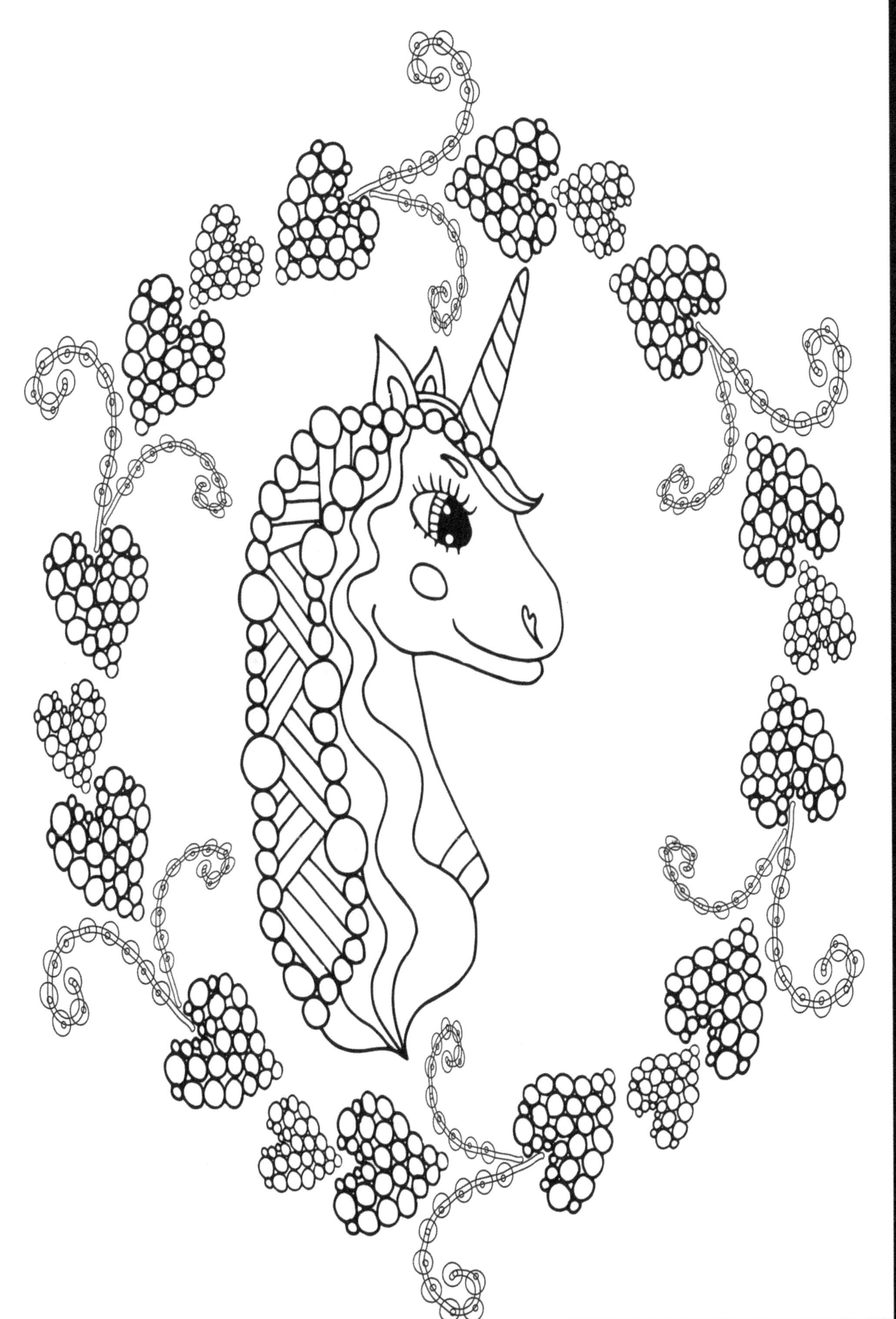

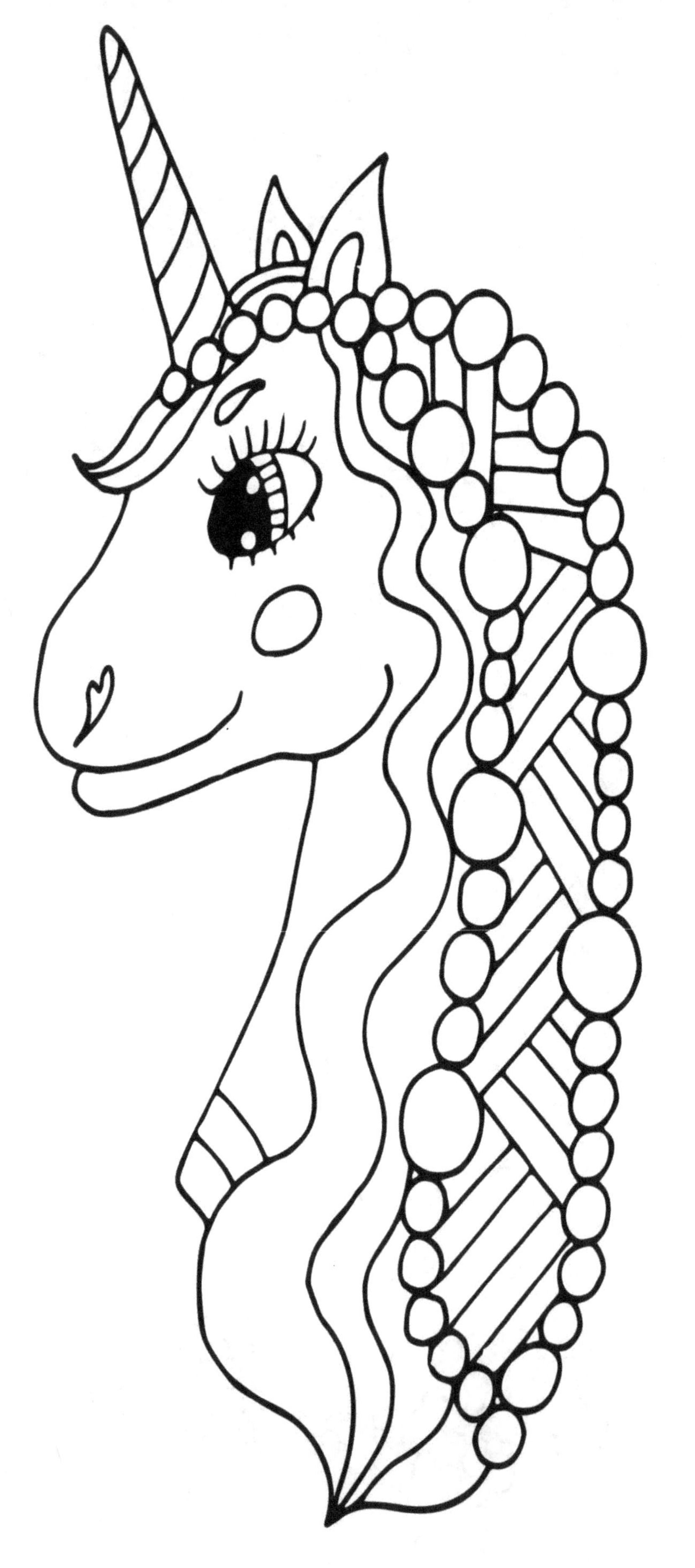

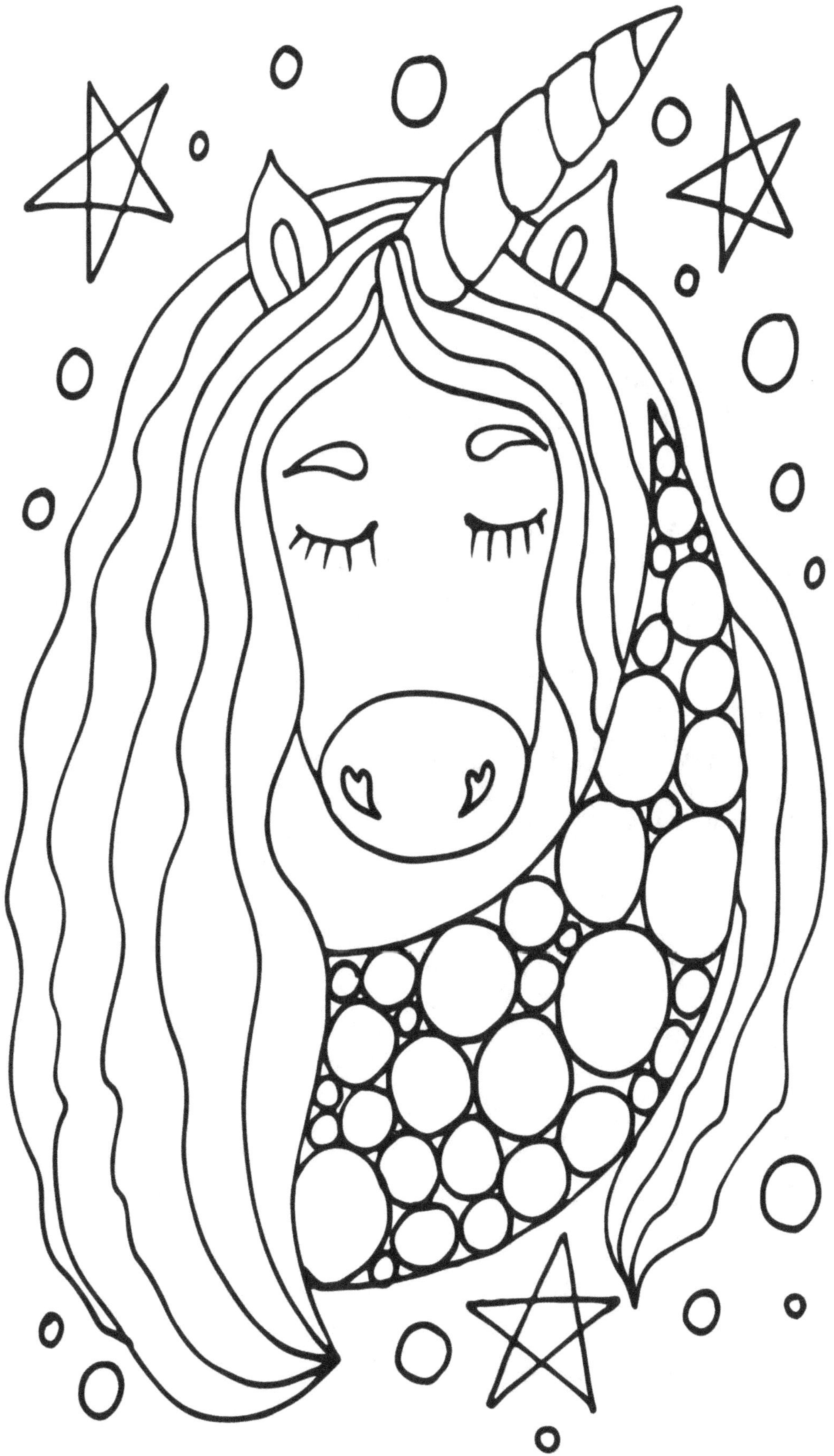

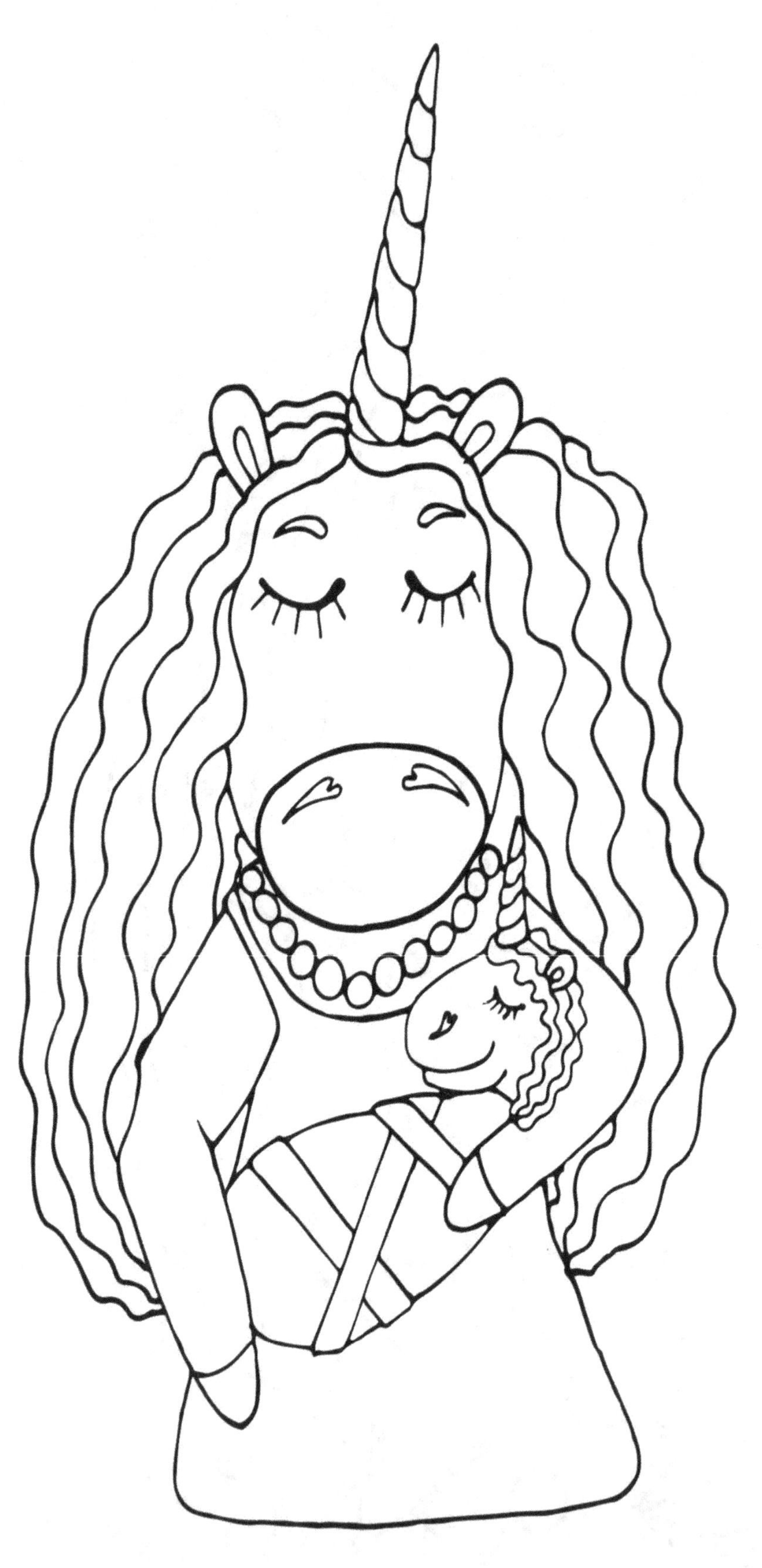

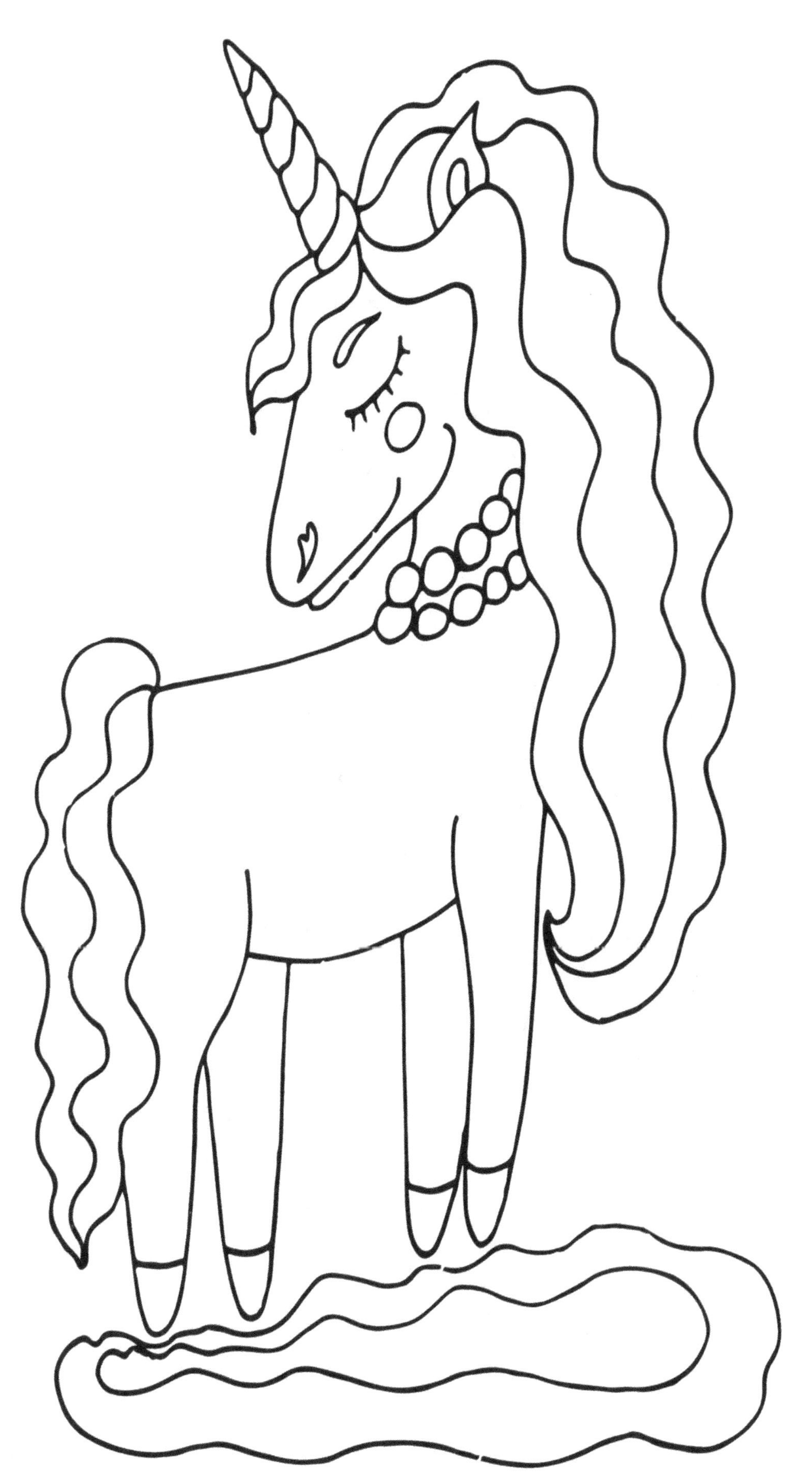

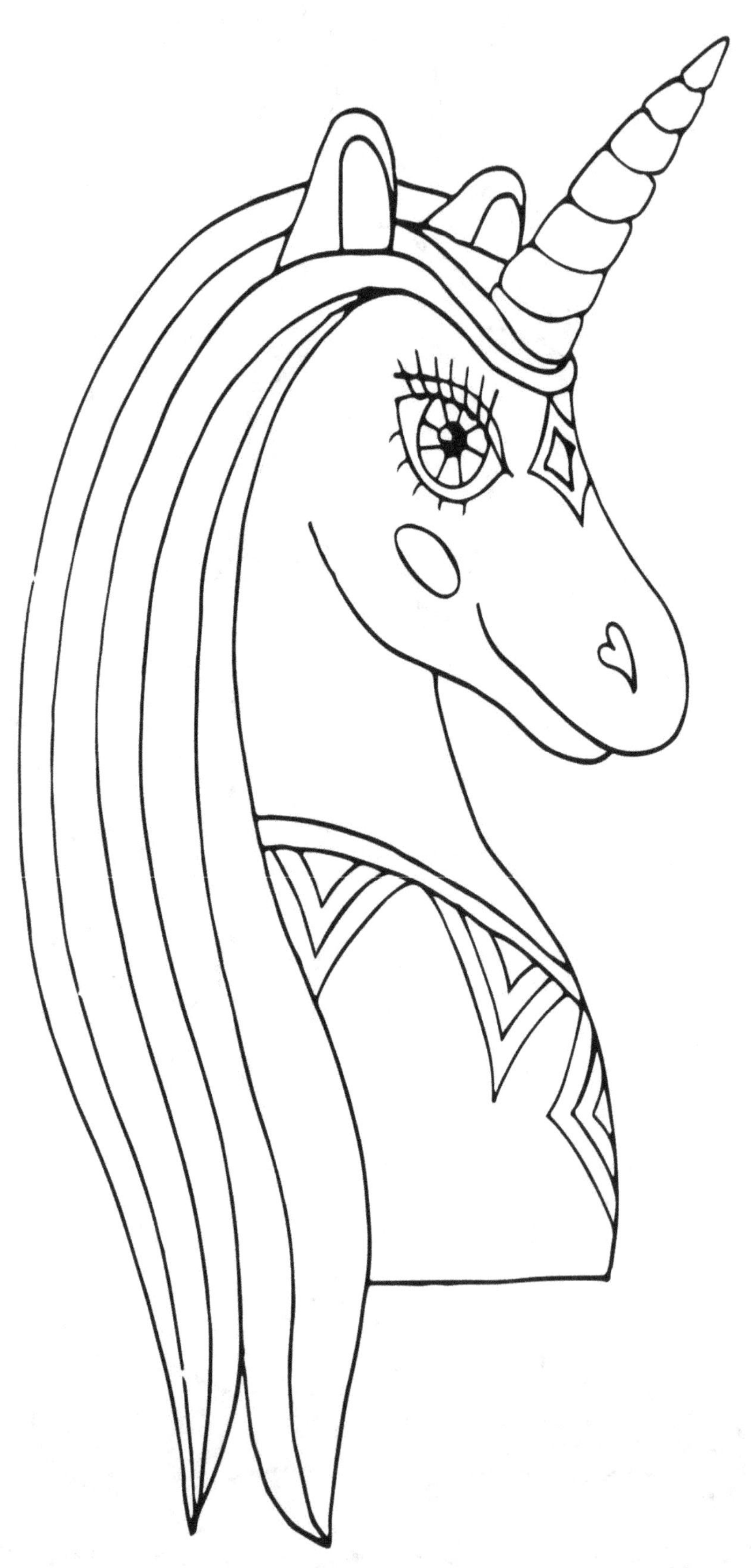

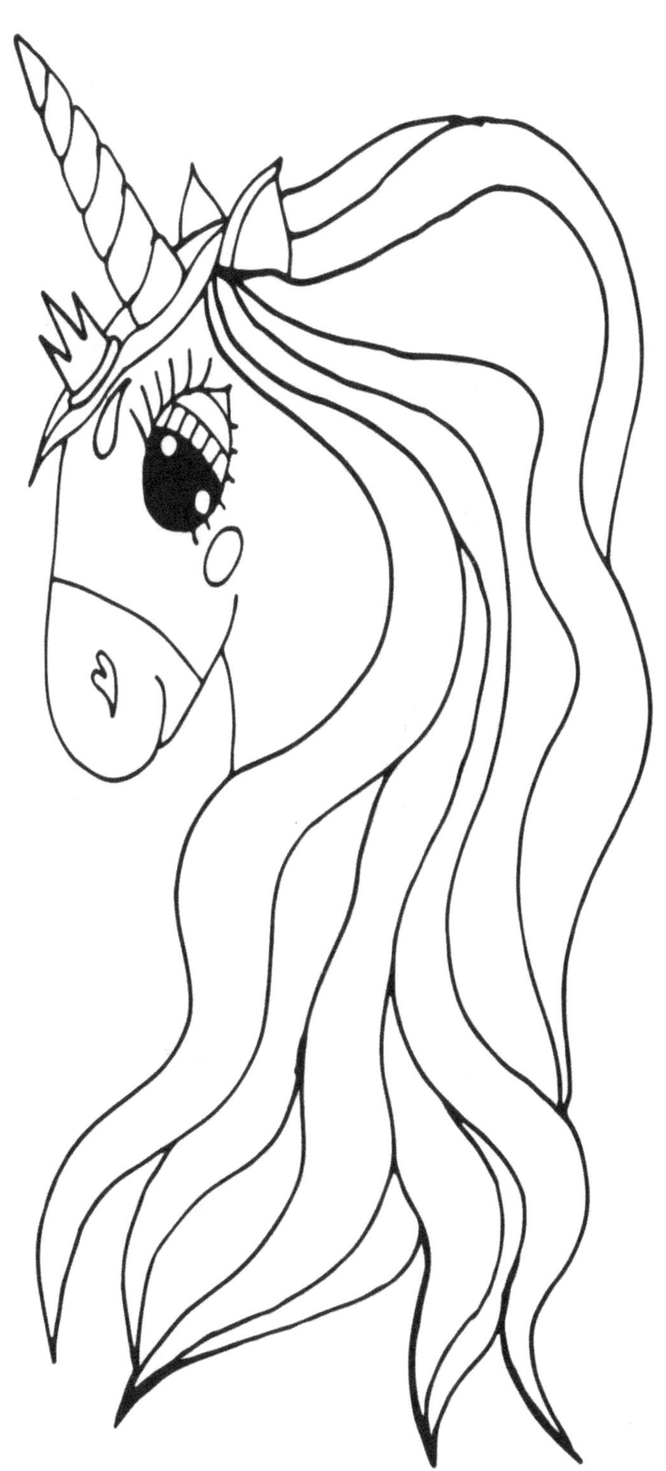

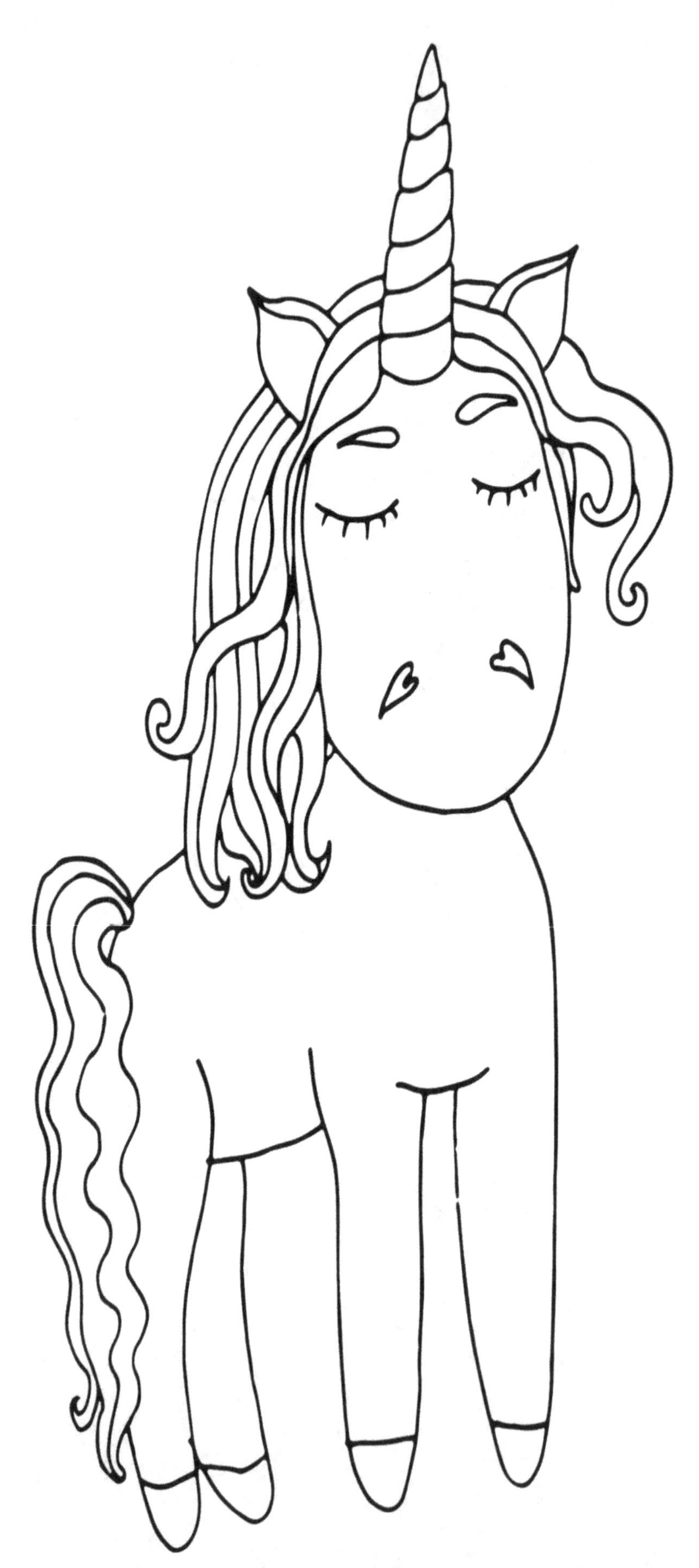

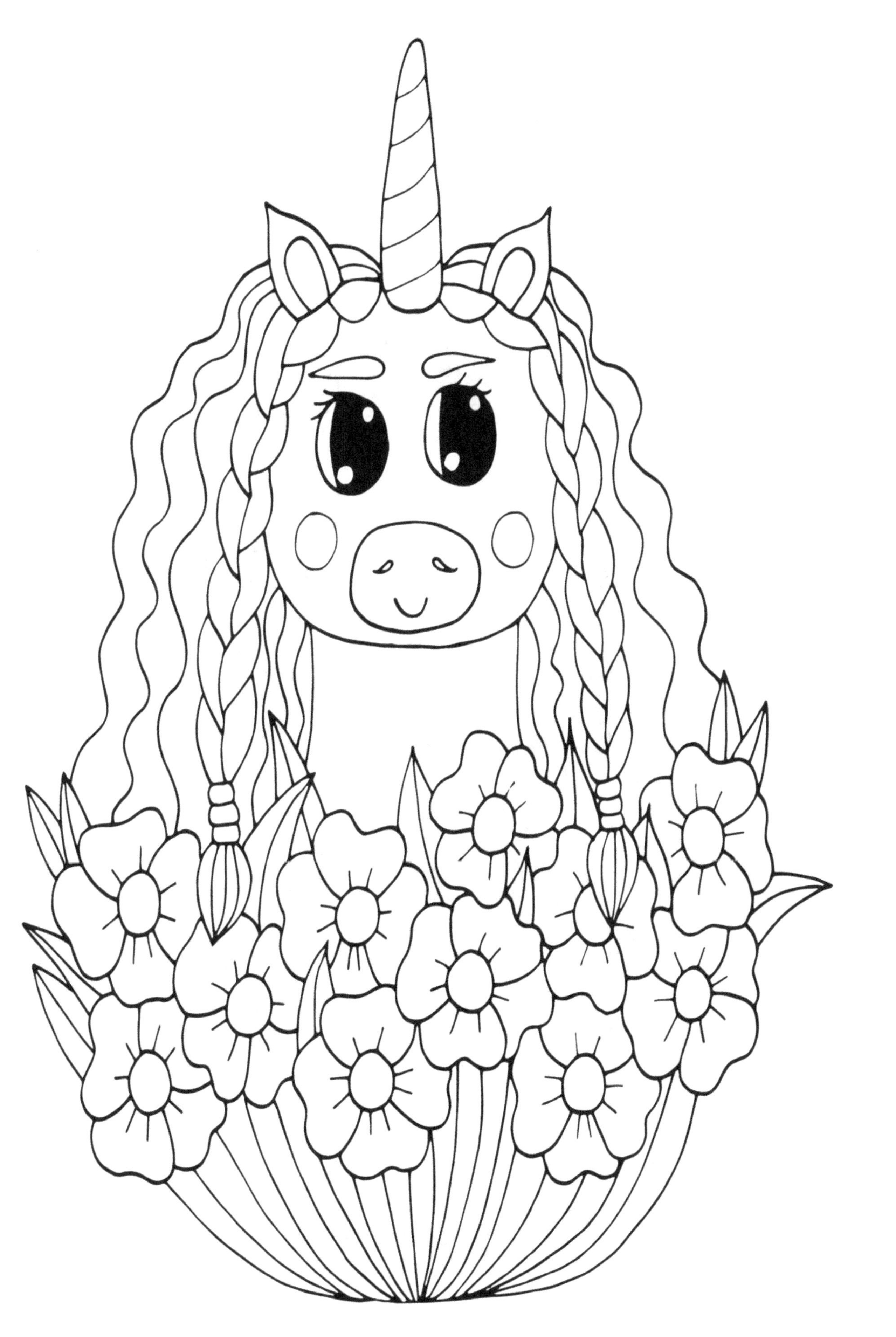

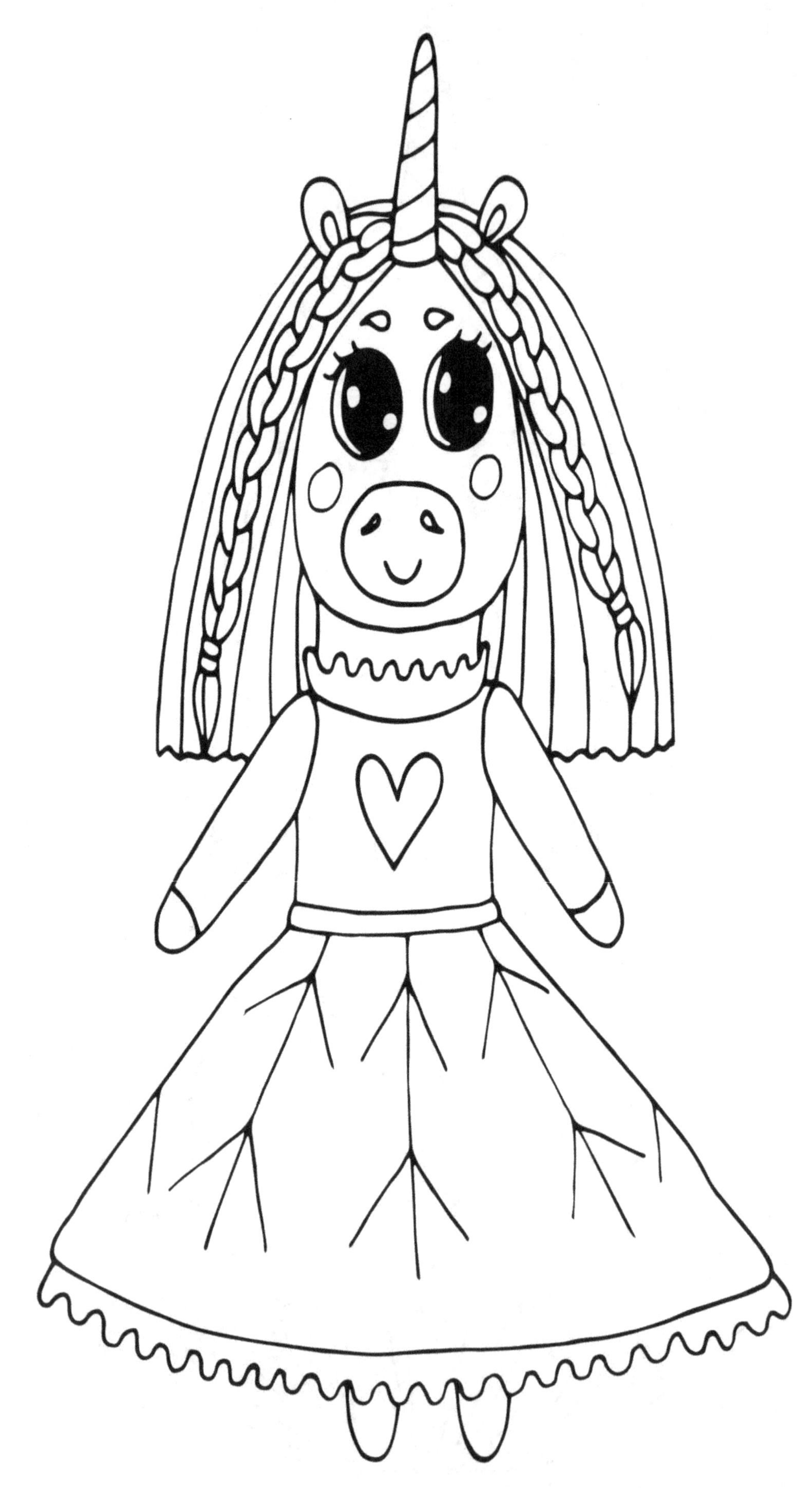

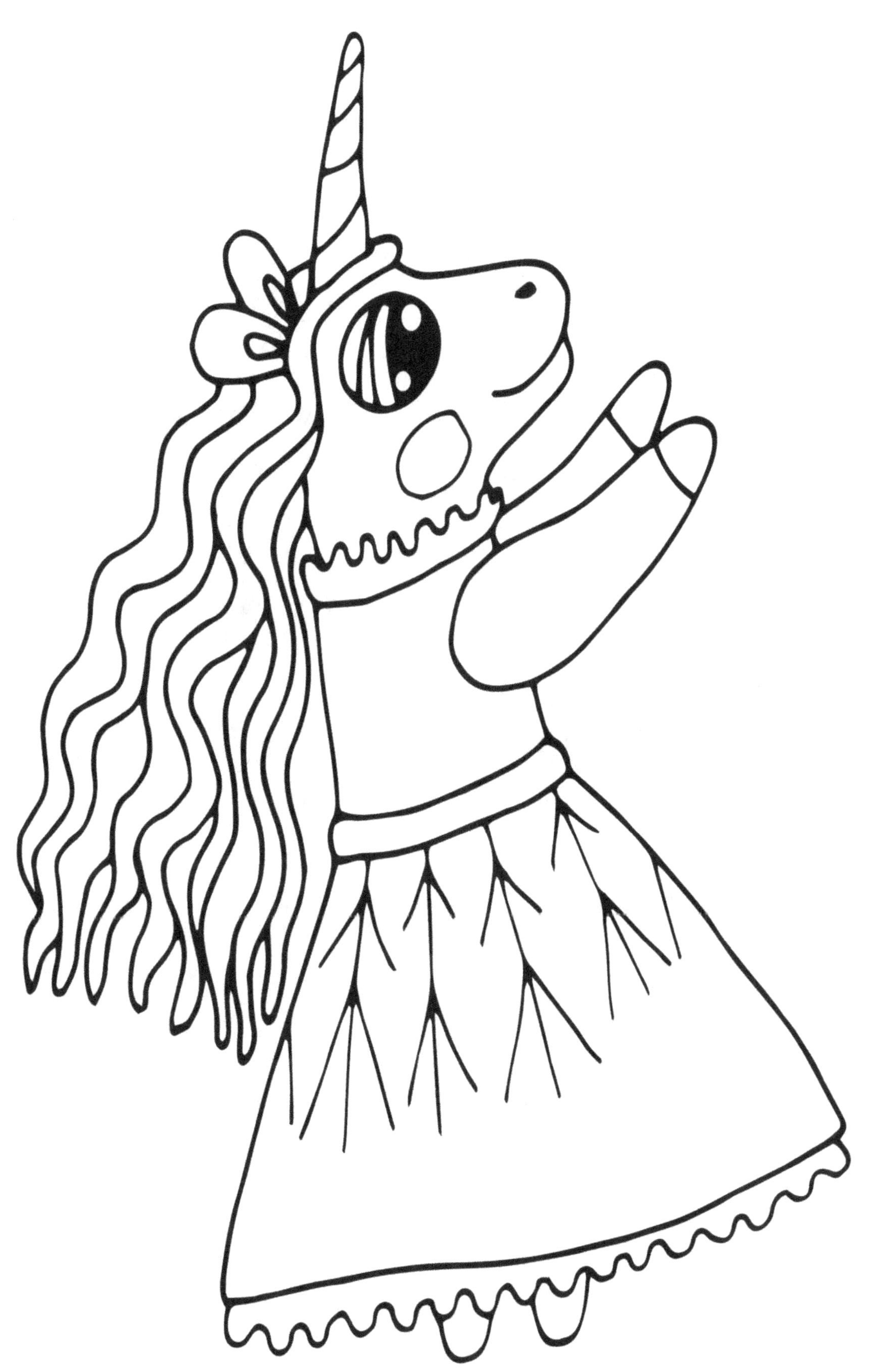

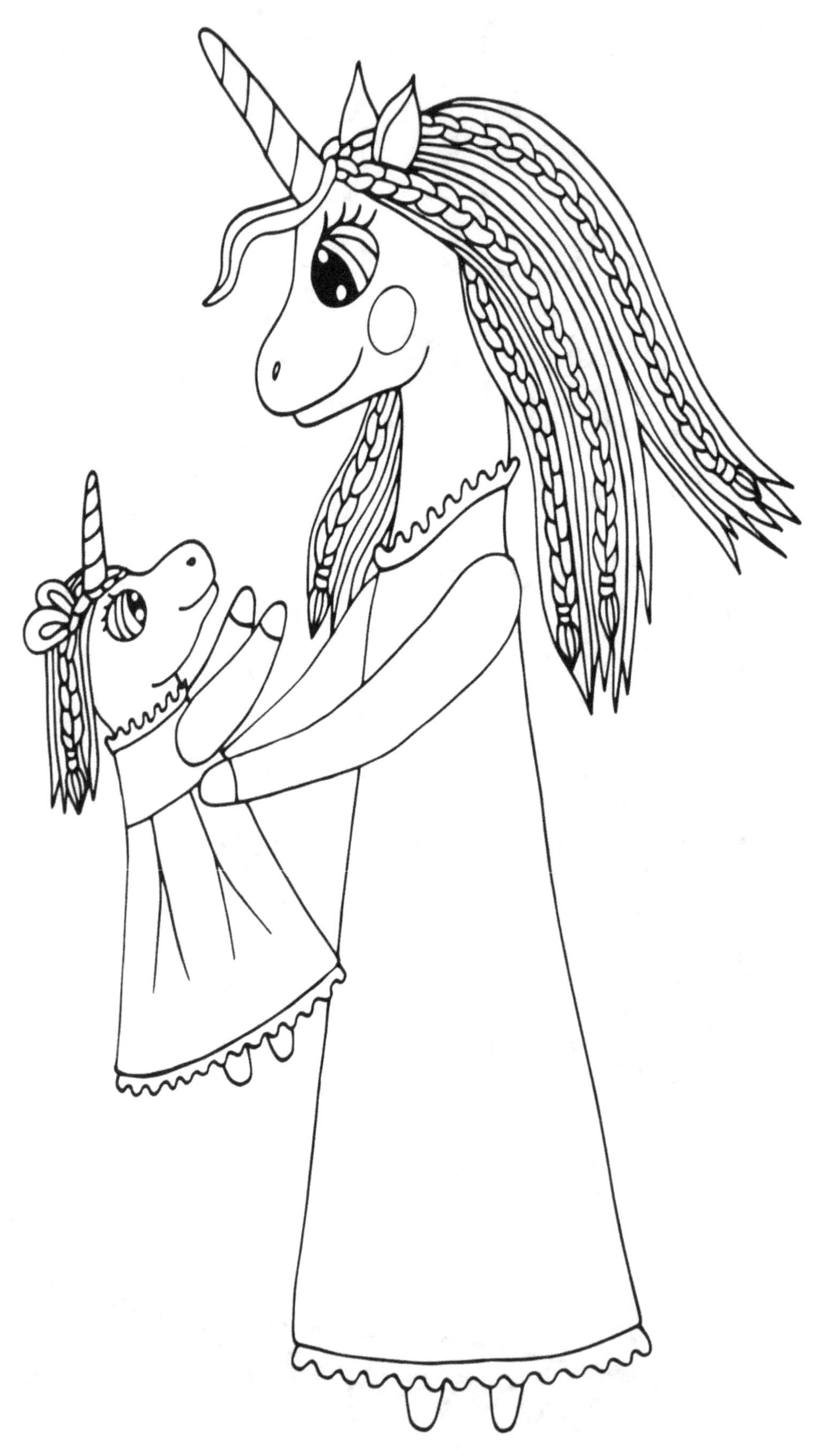

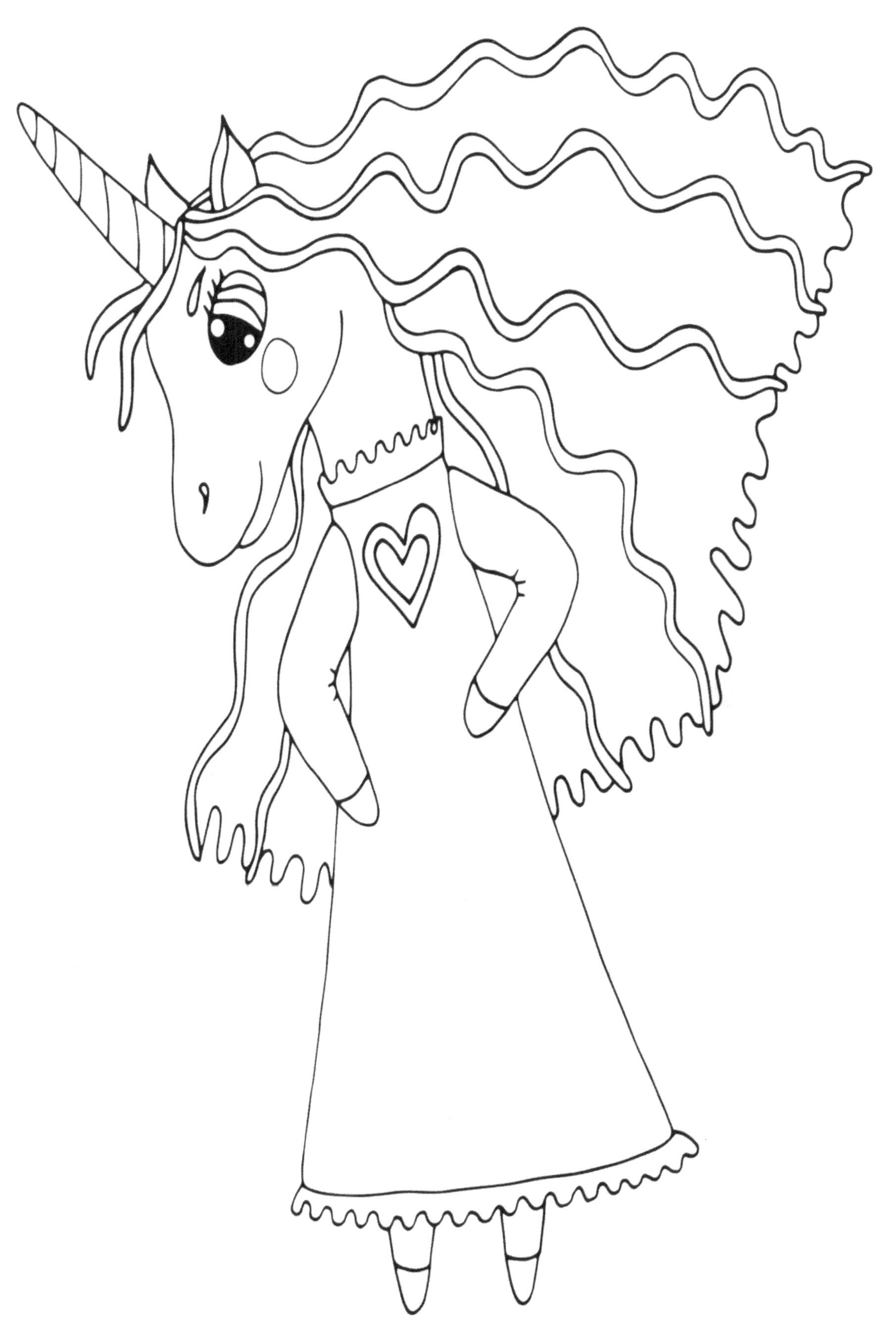

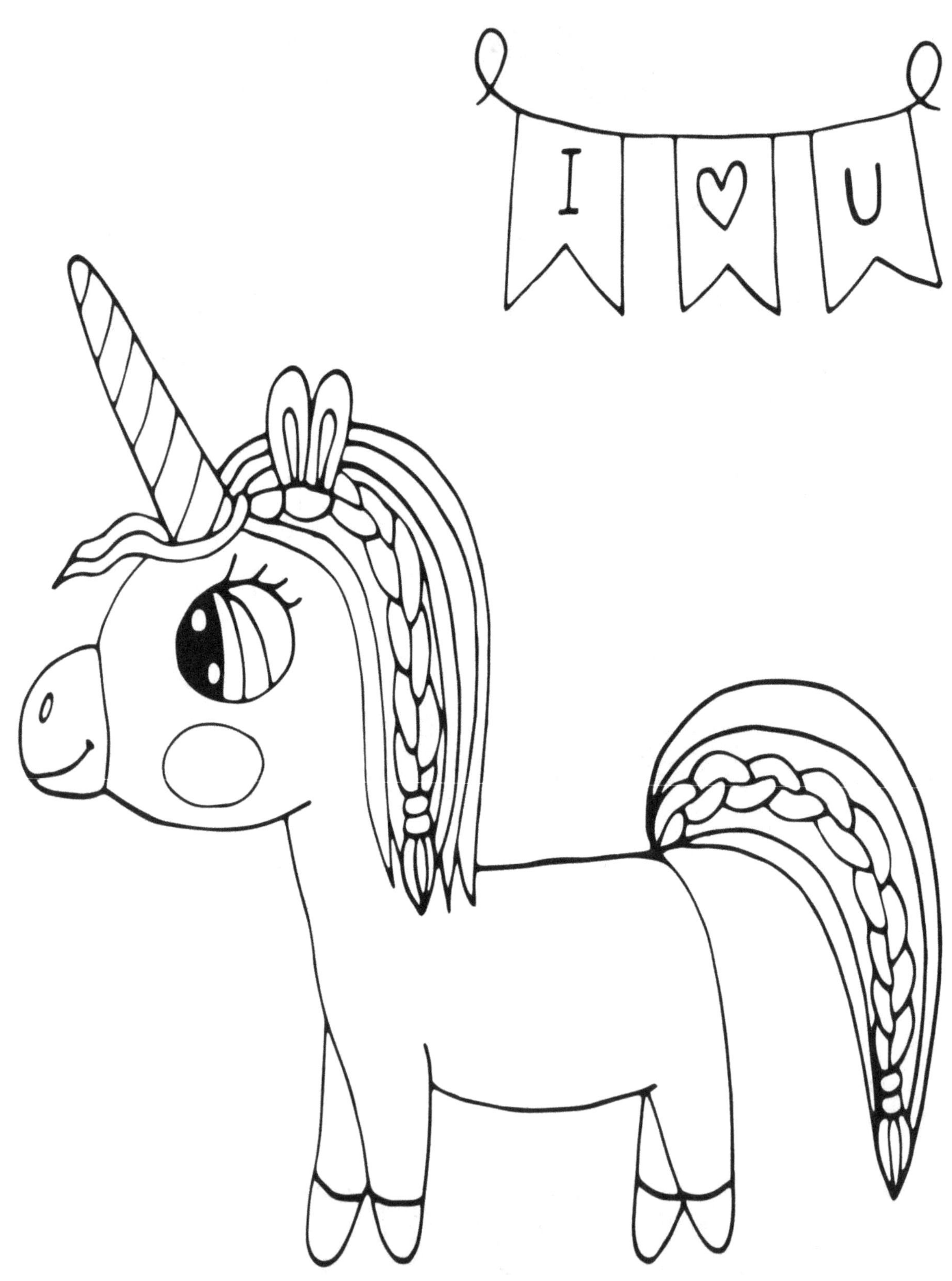
I ♡ U

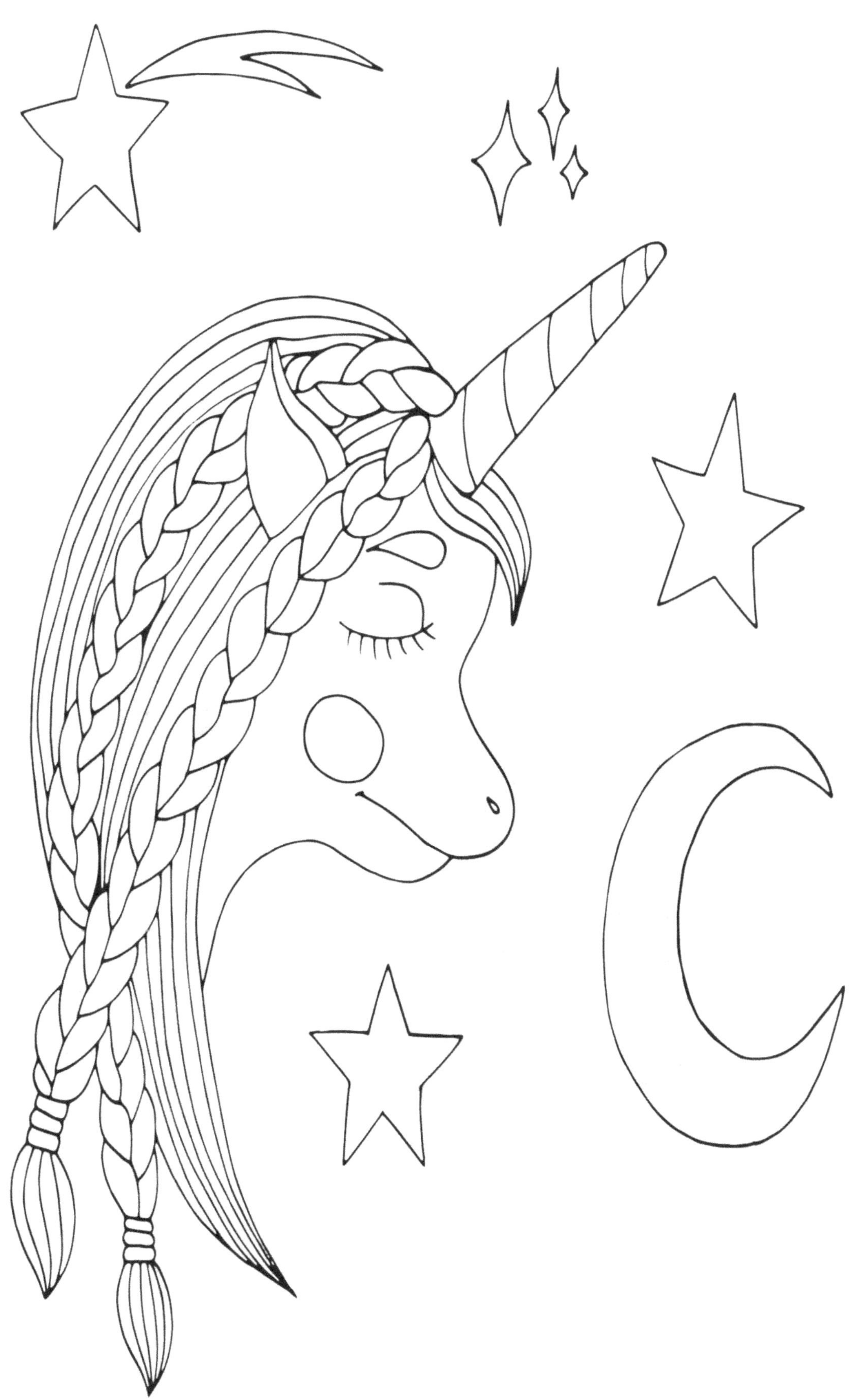

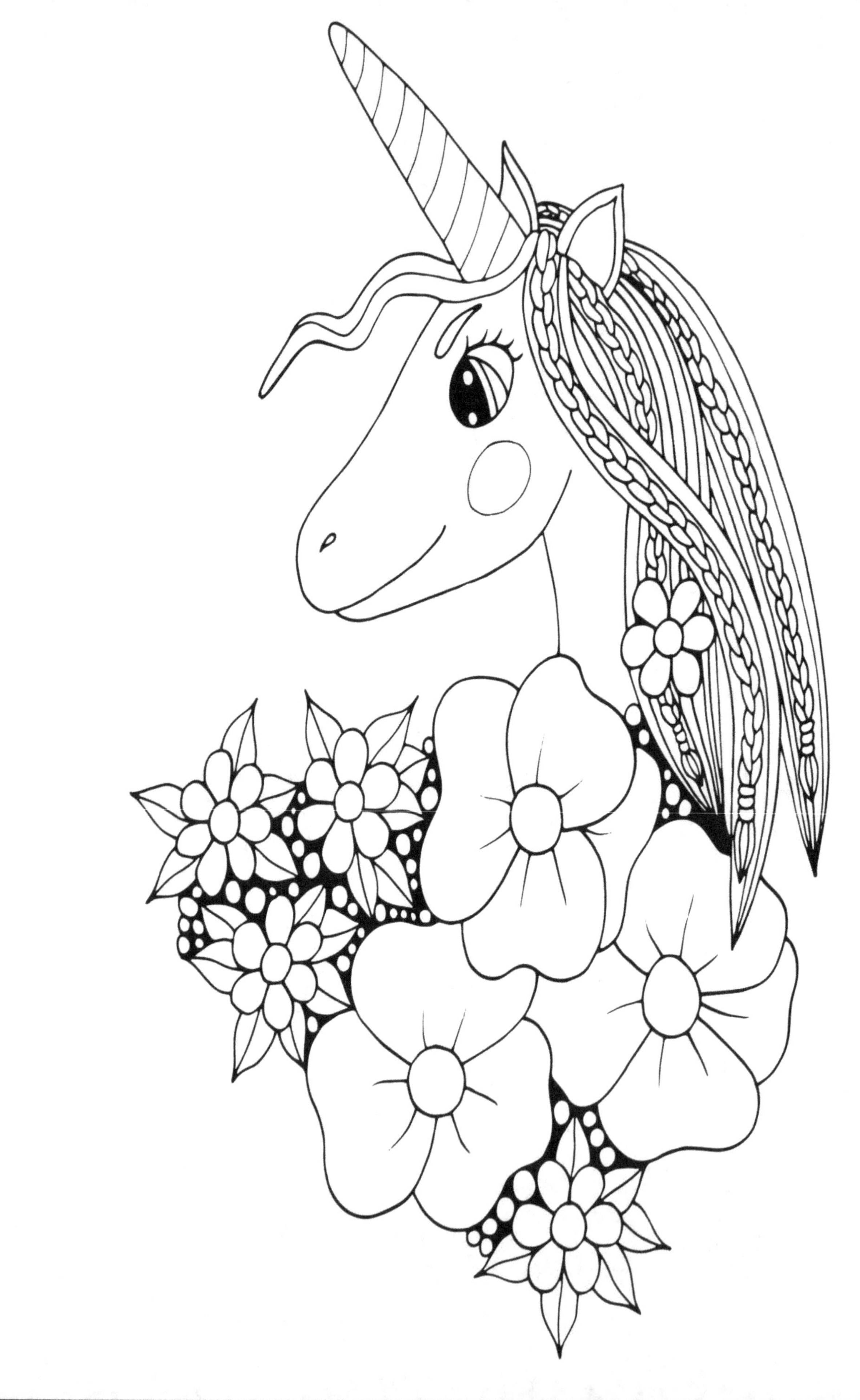

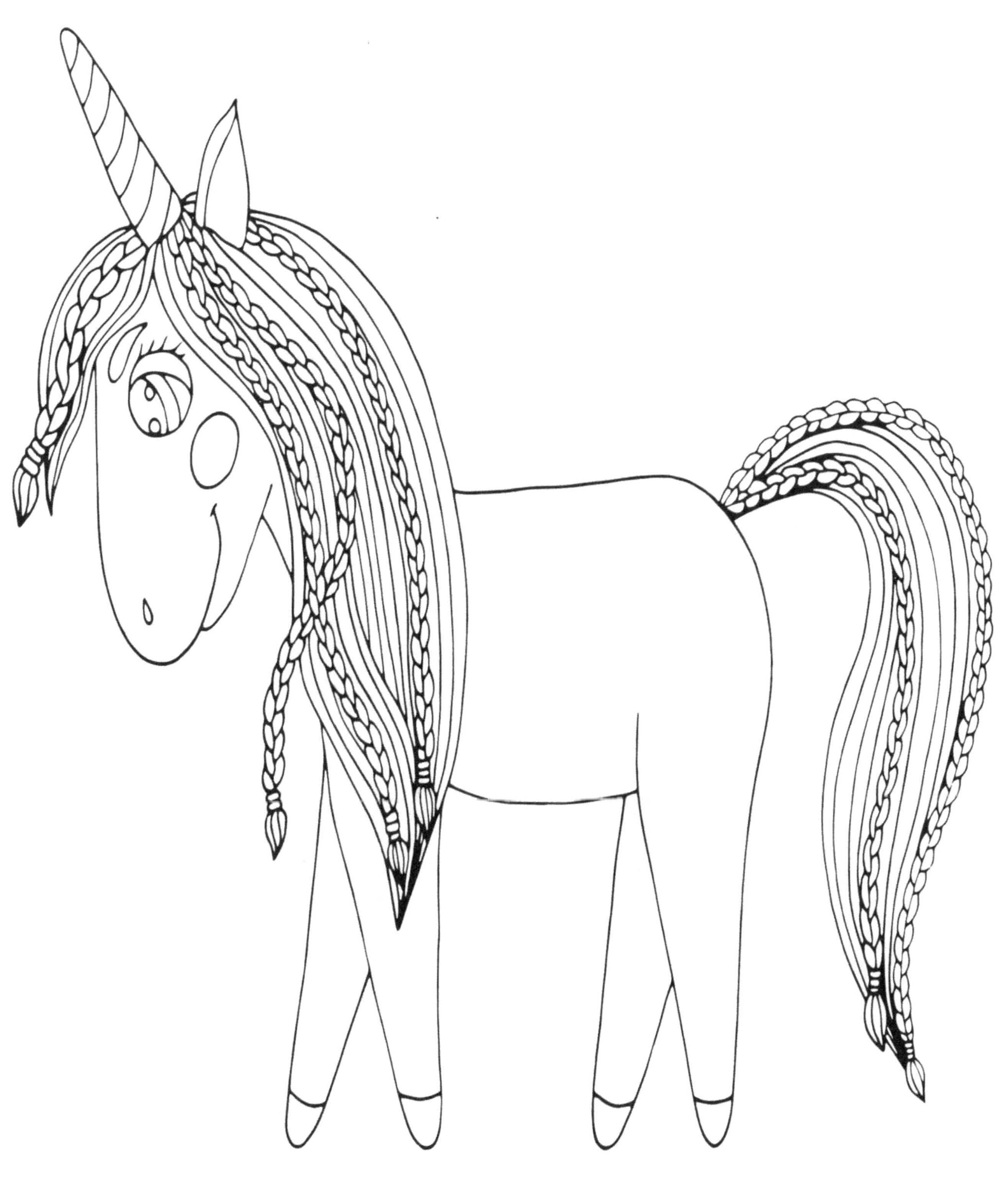

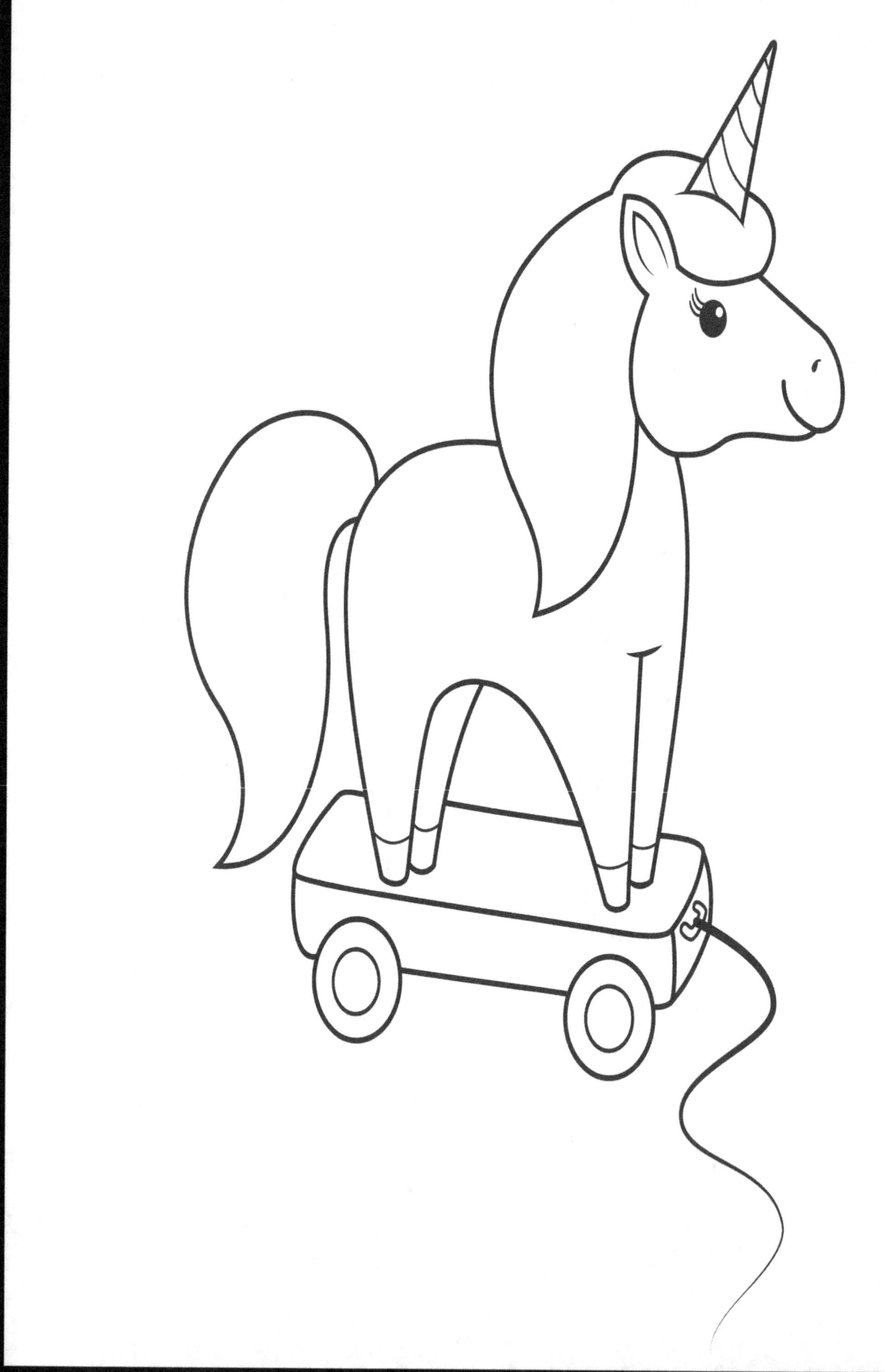

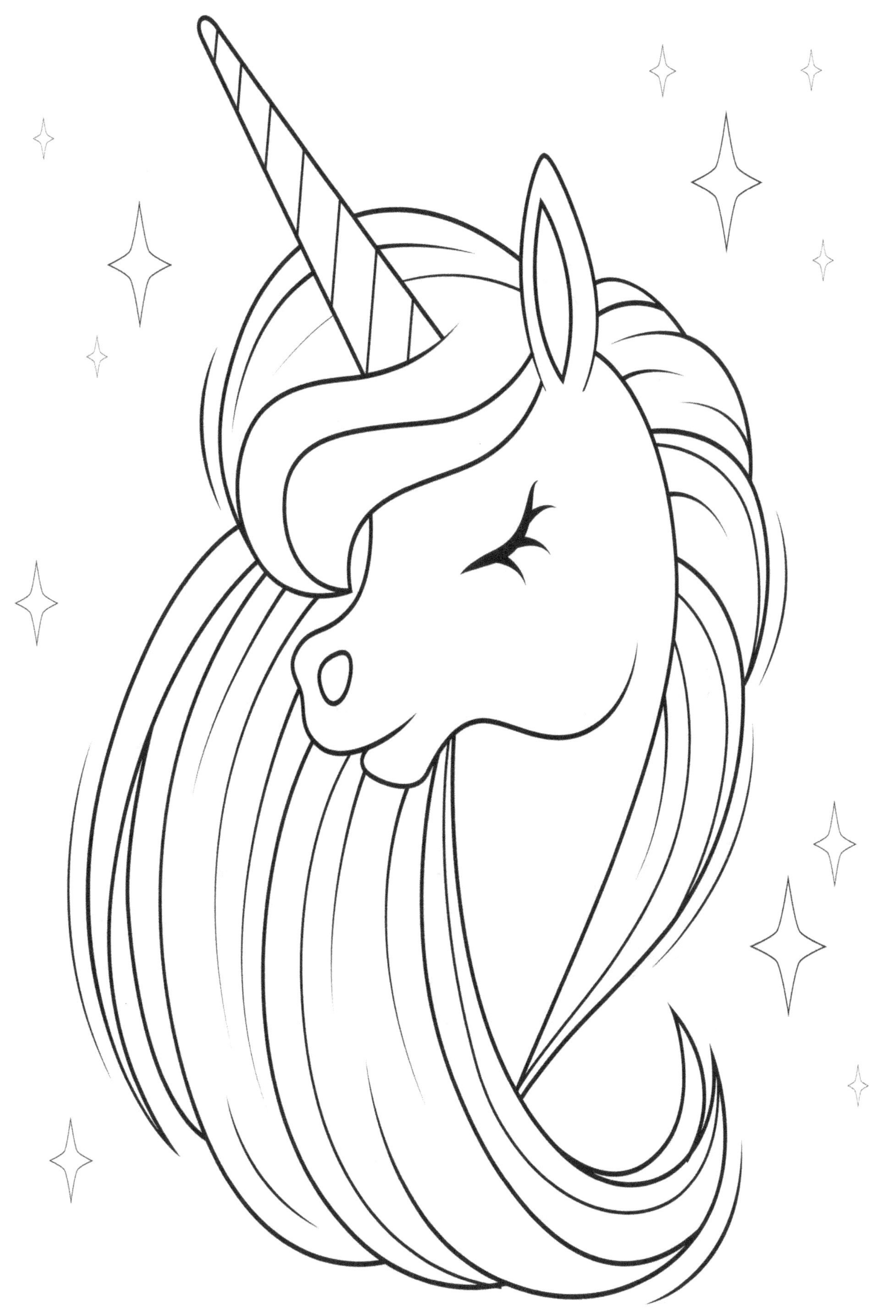

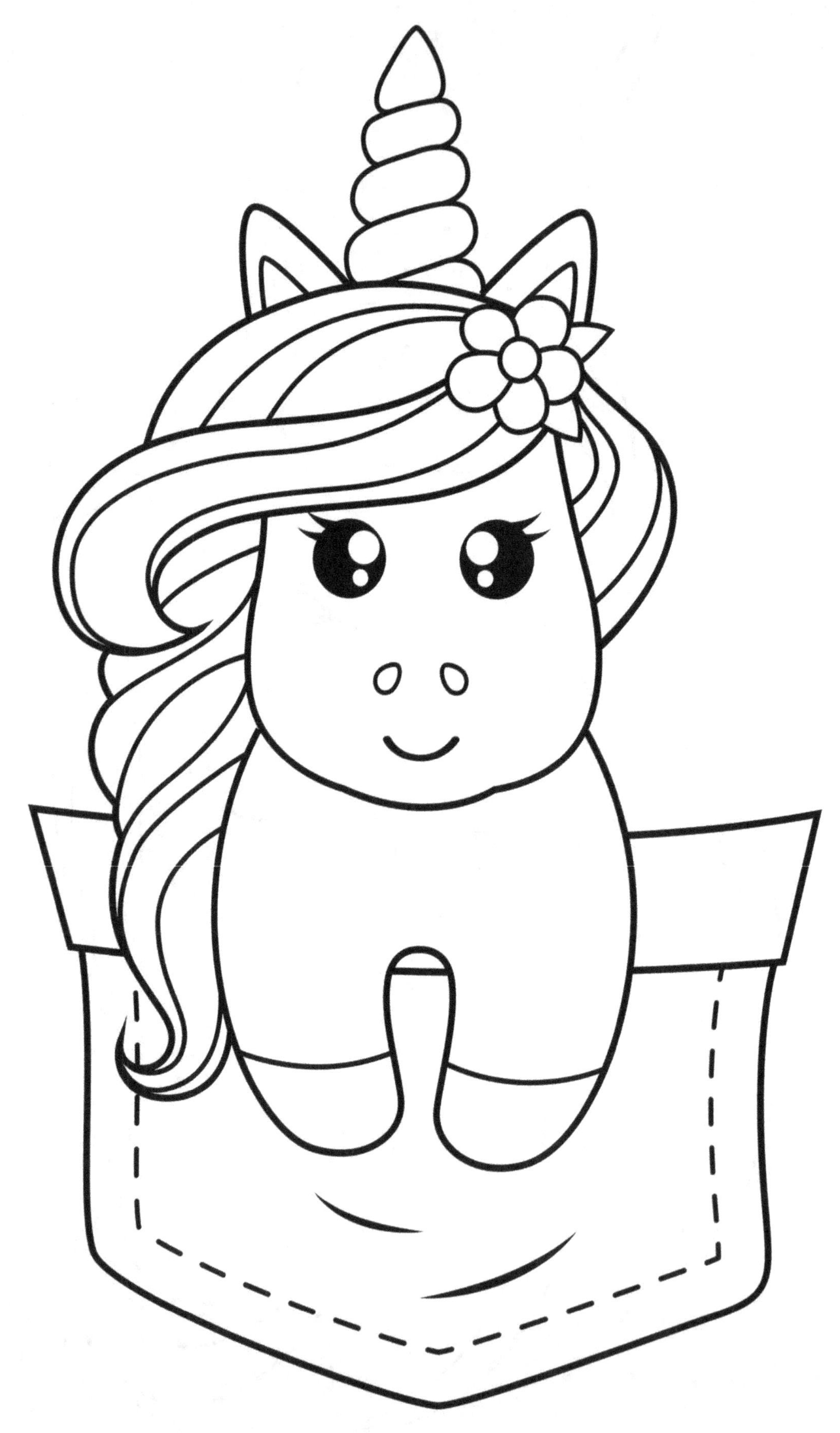

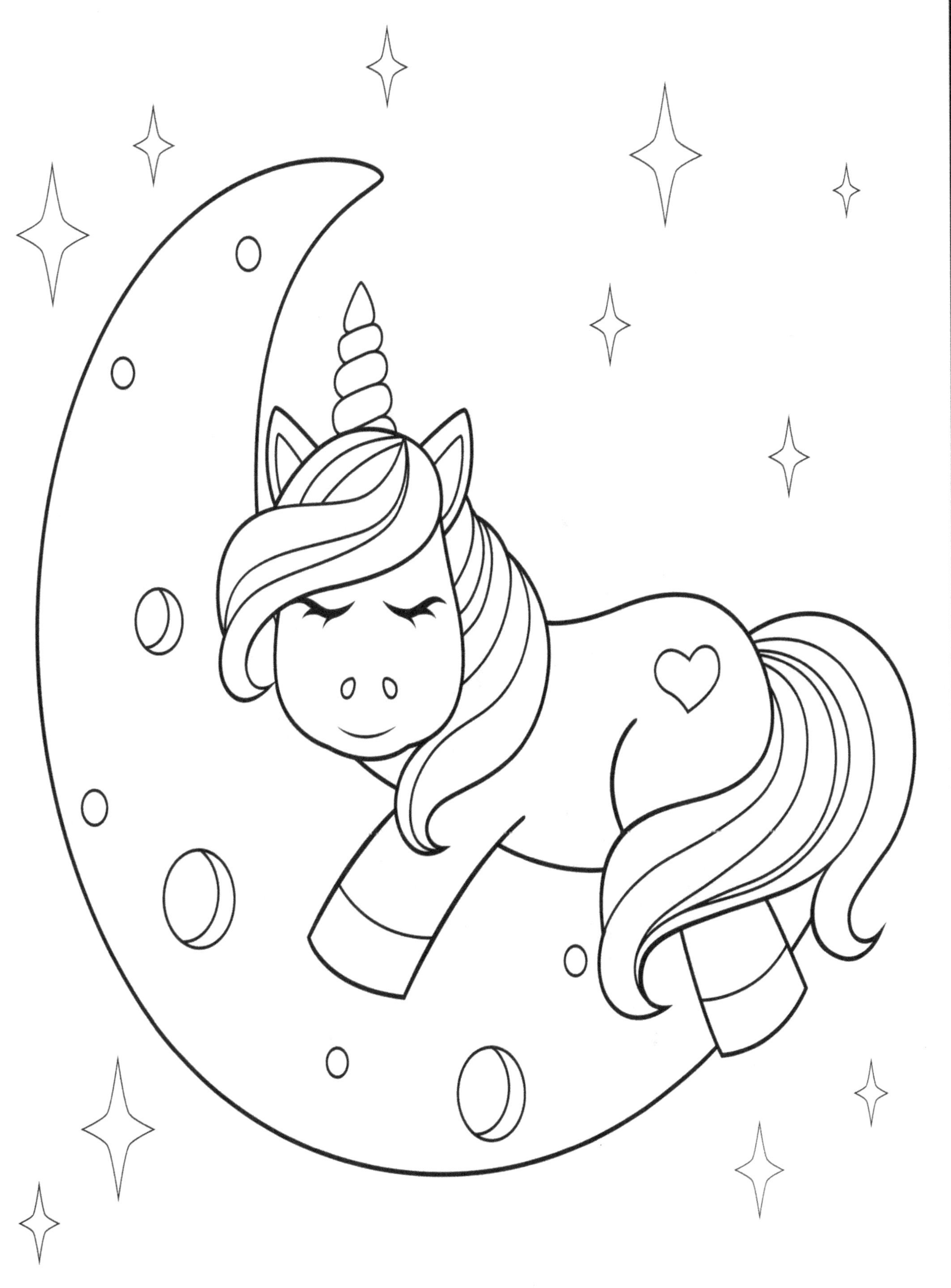

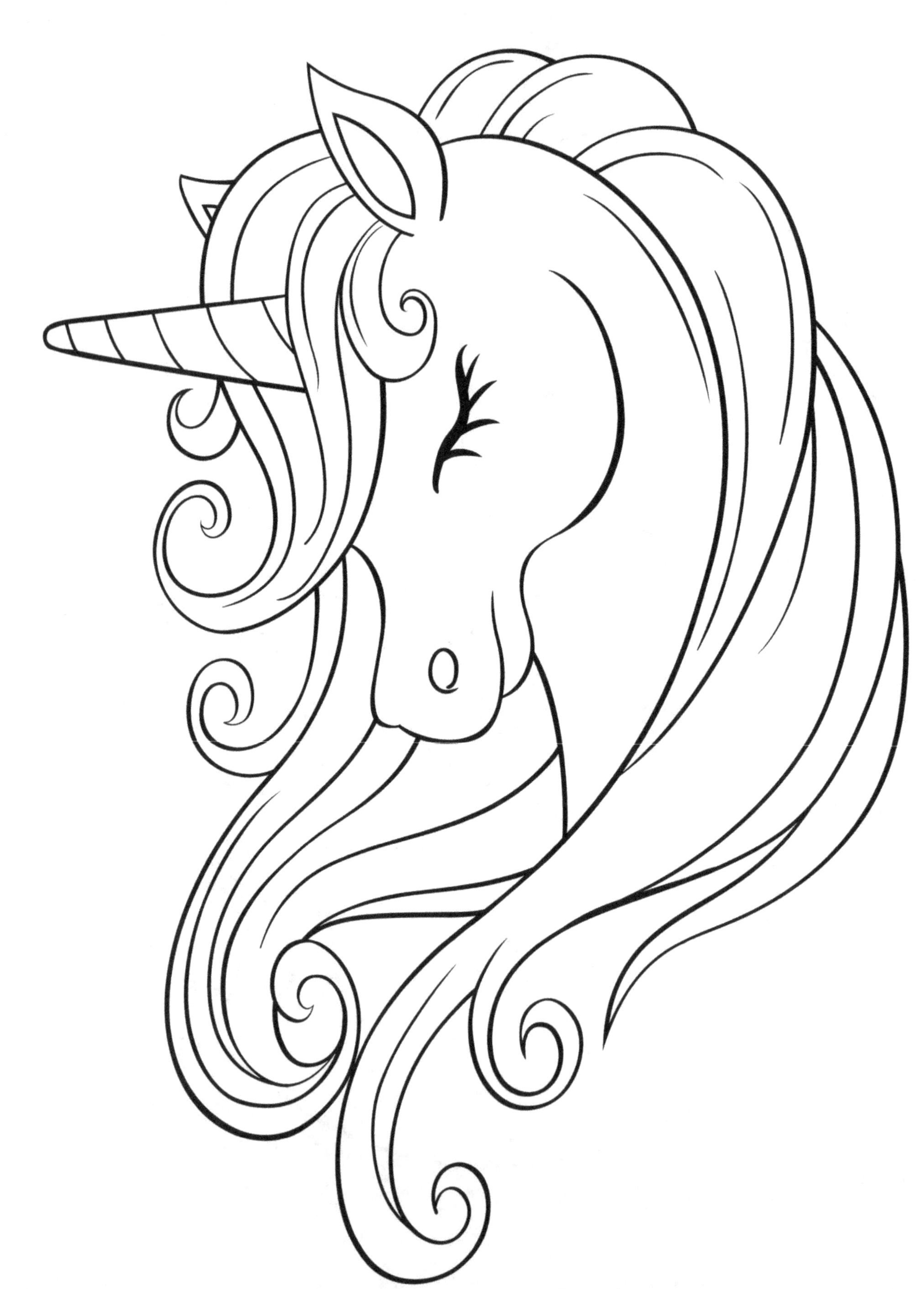

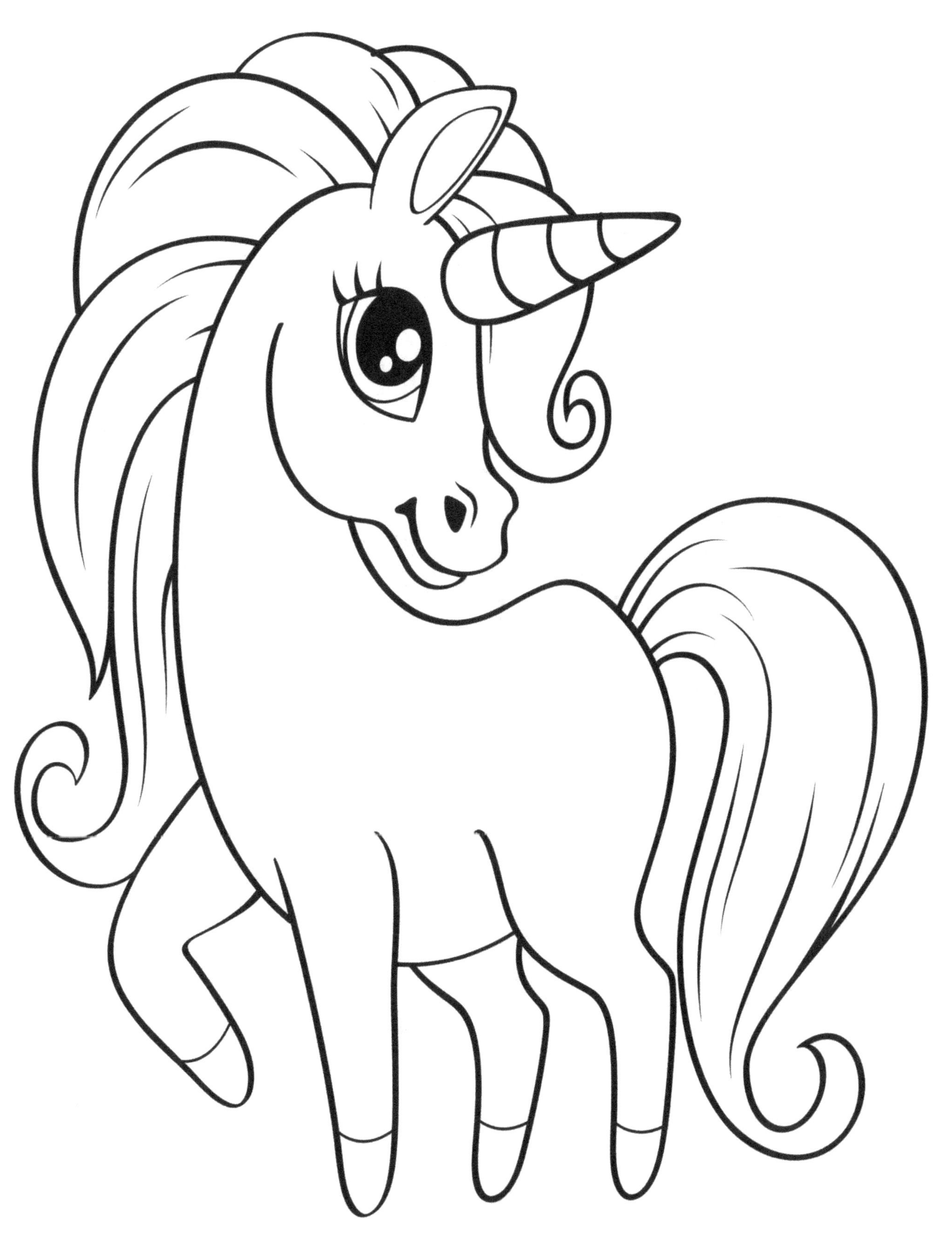

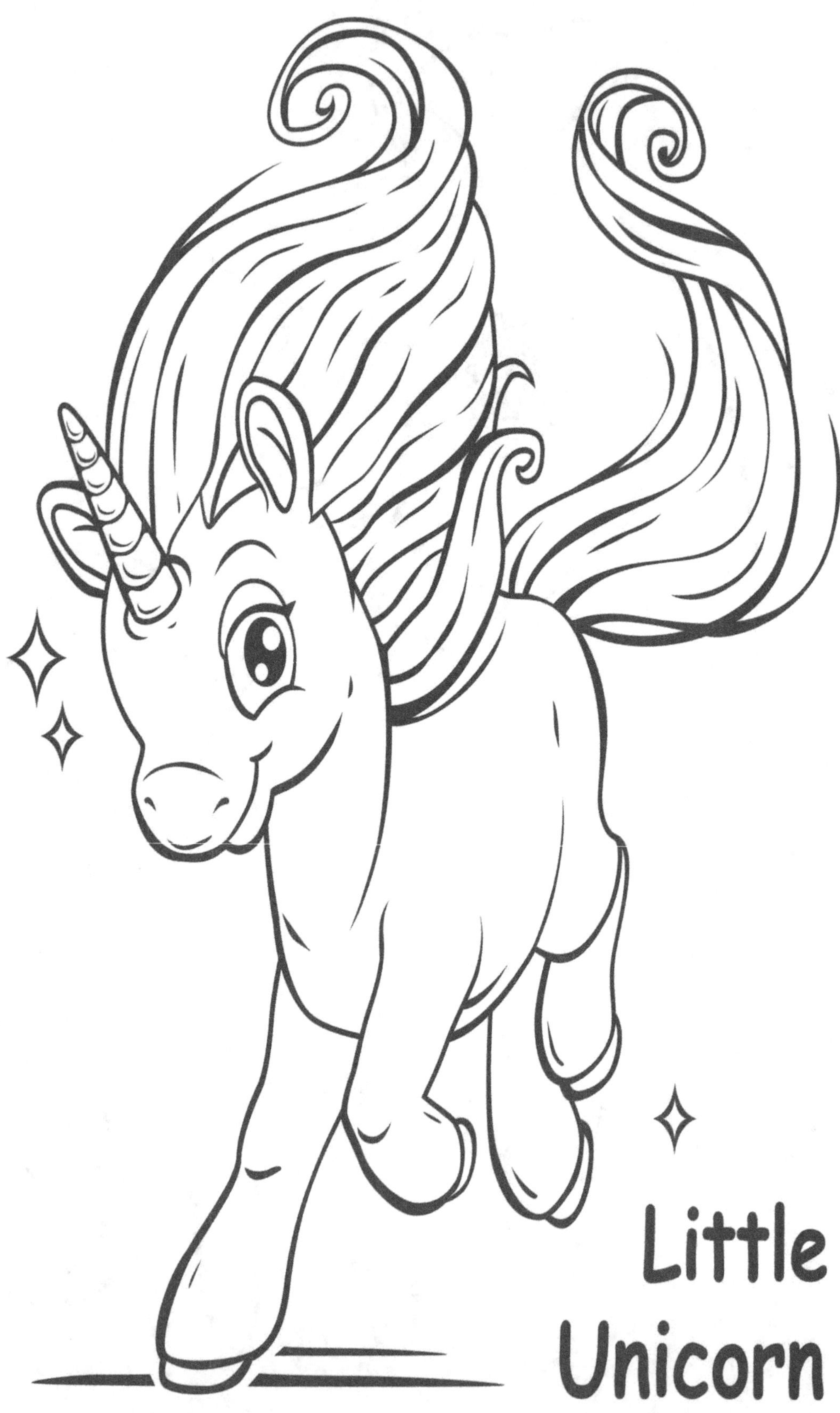

Little
Unicorn

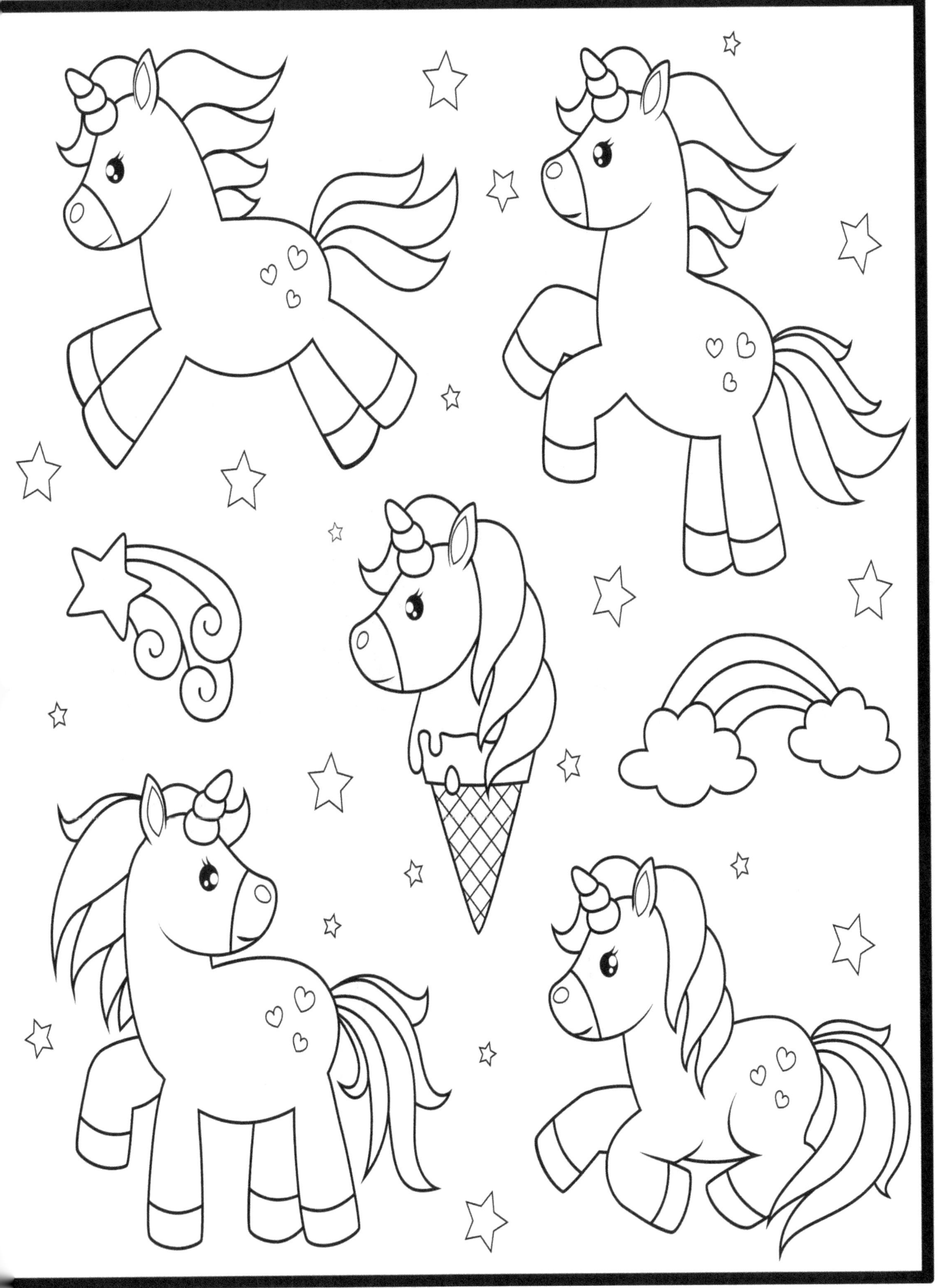

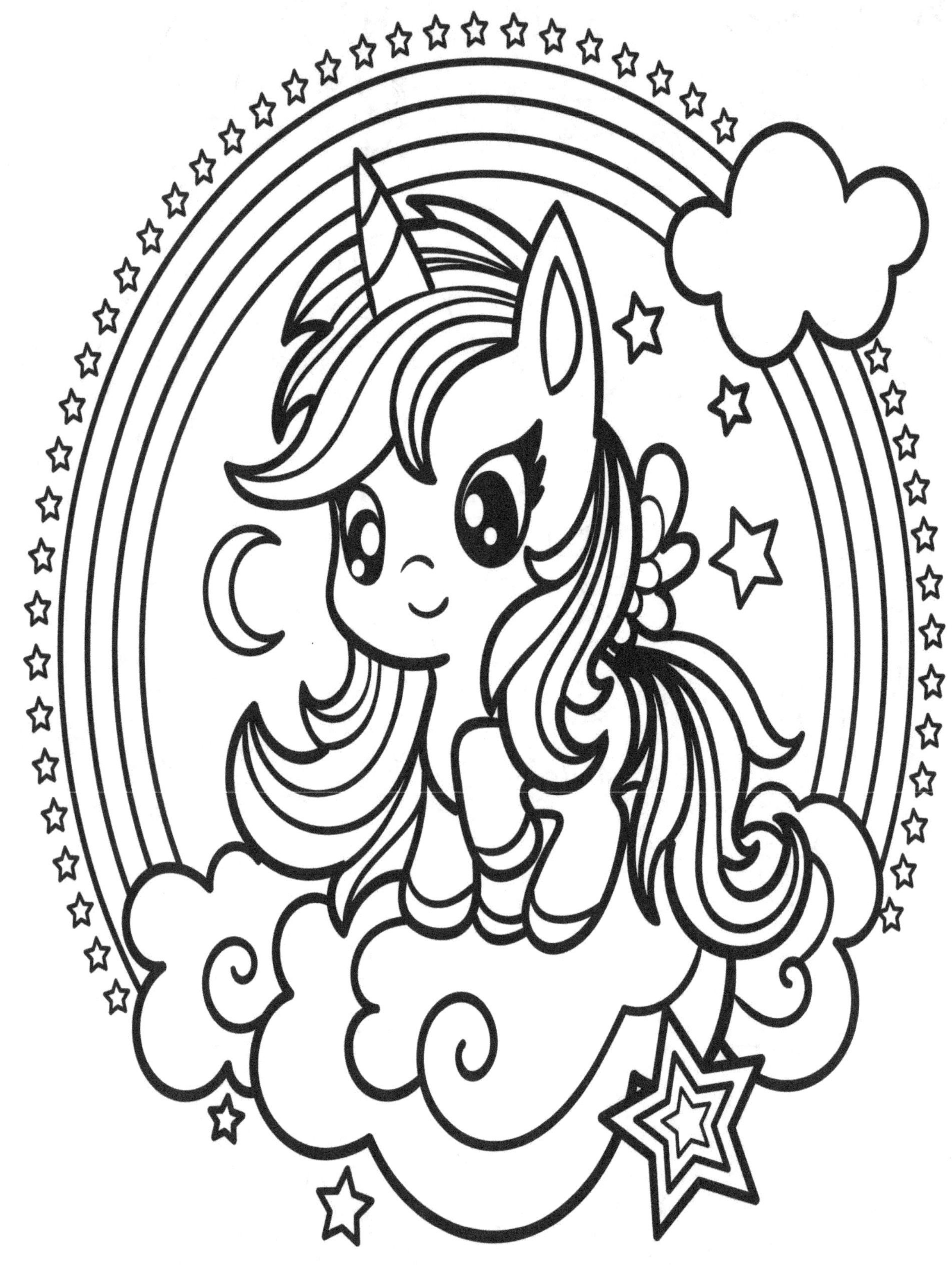

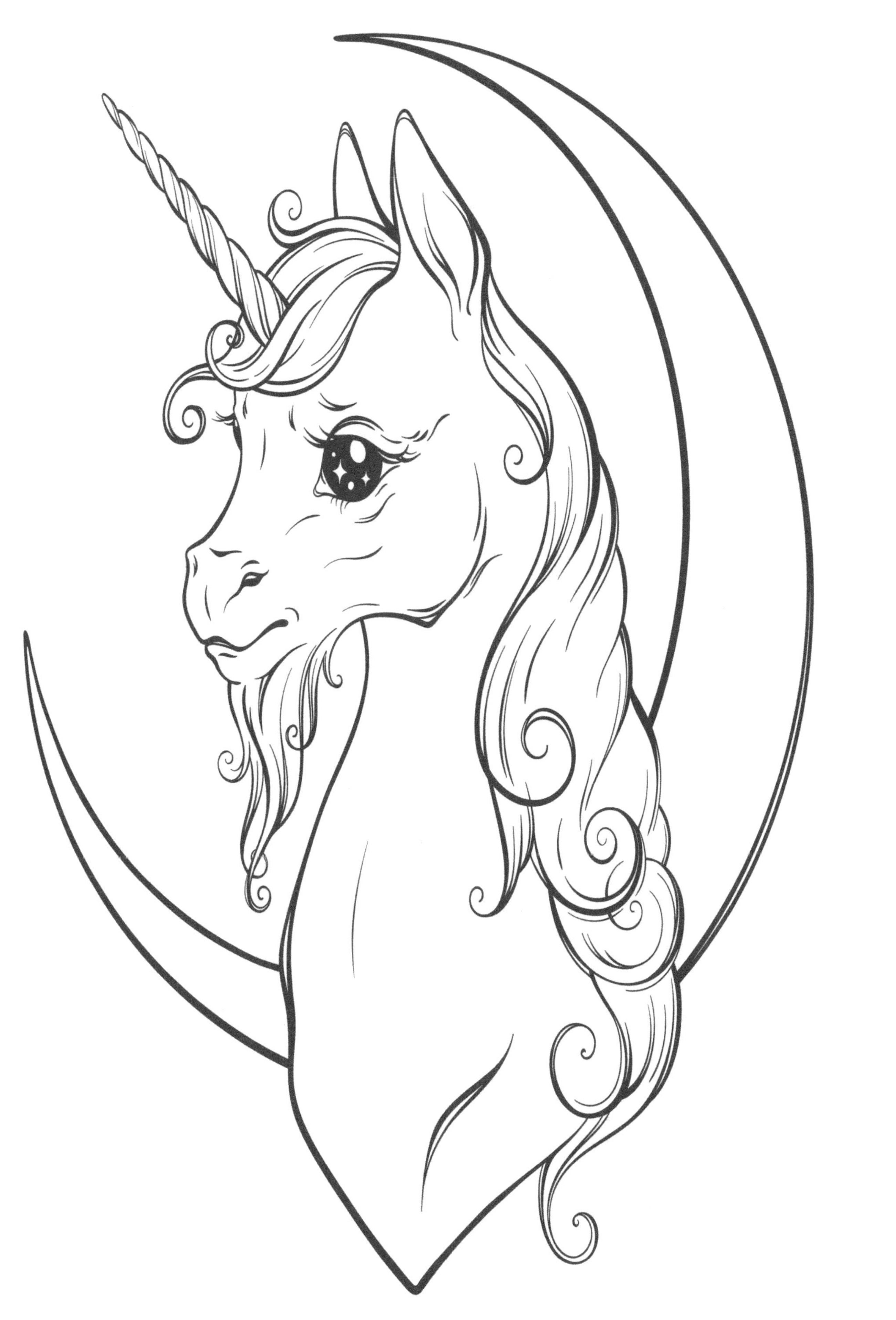

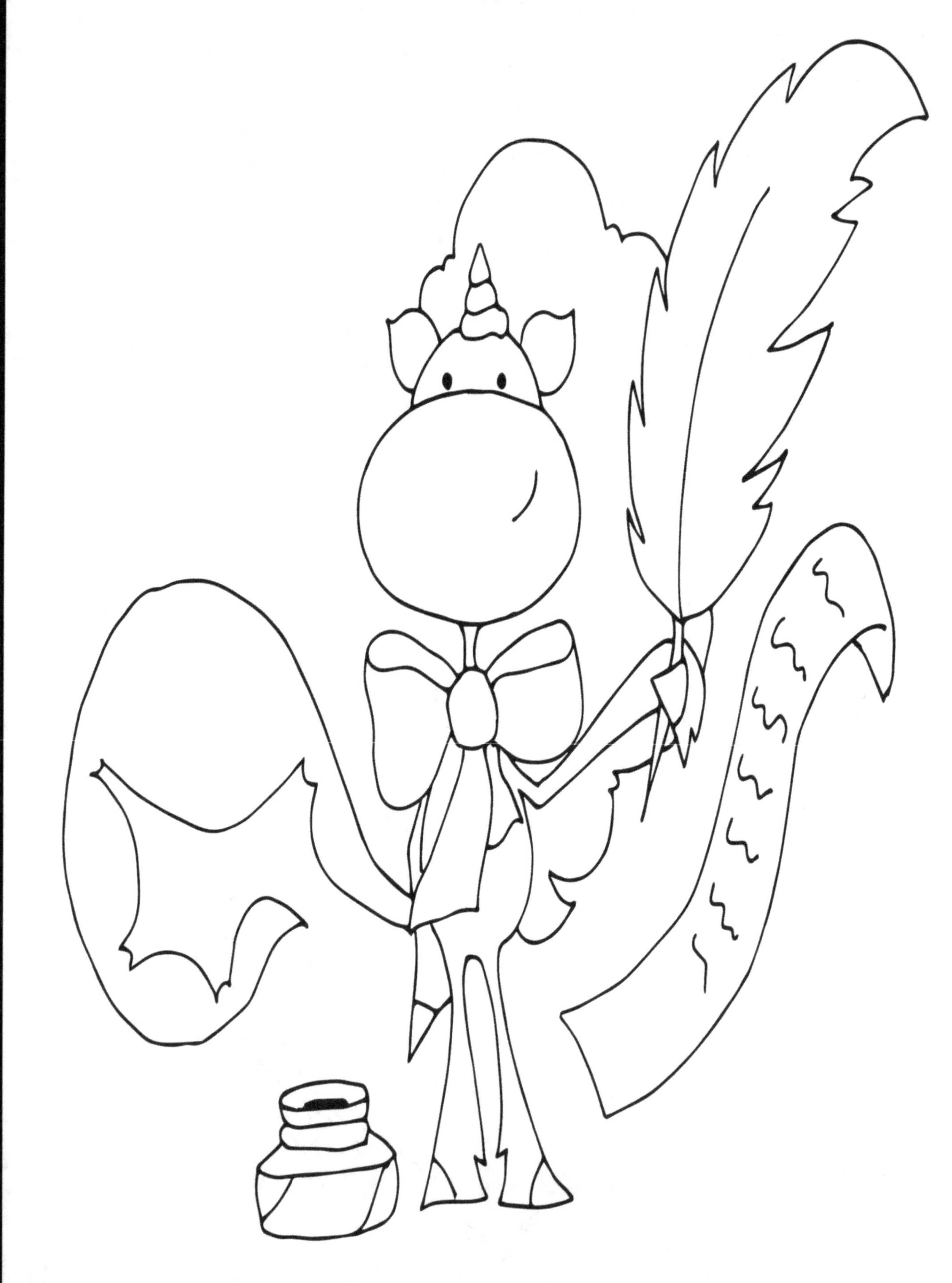

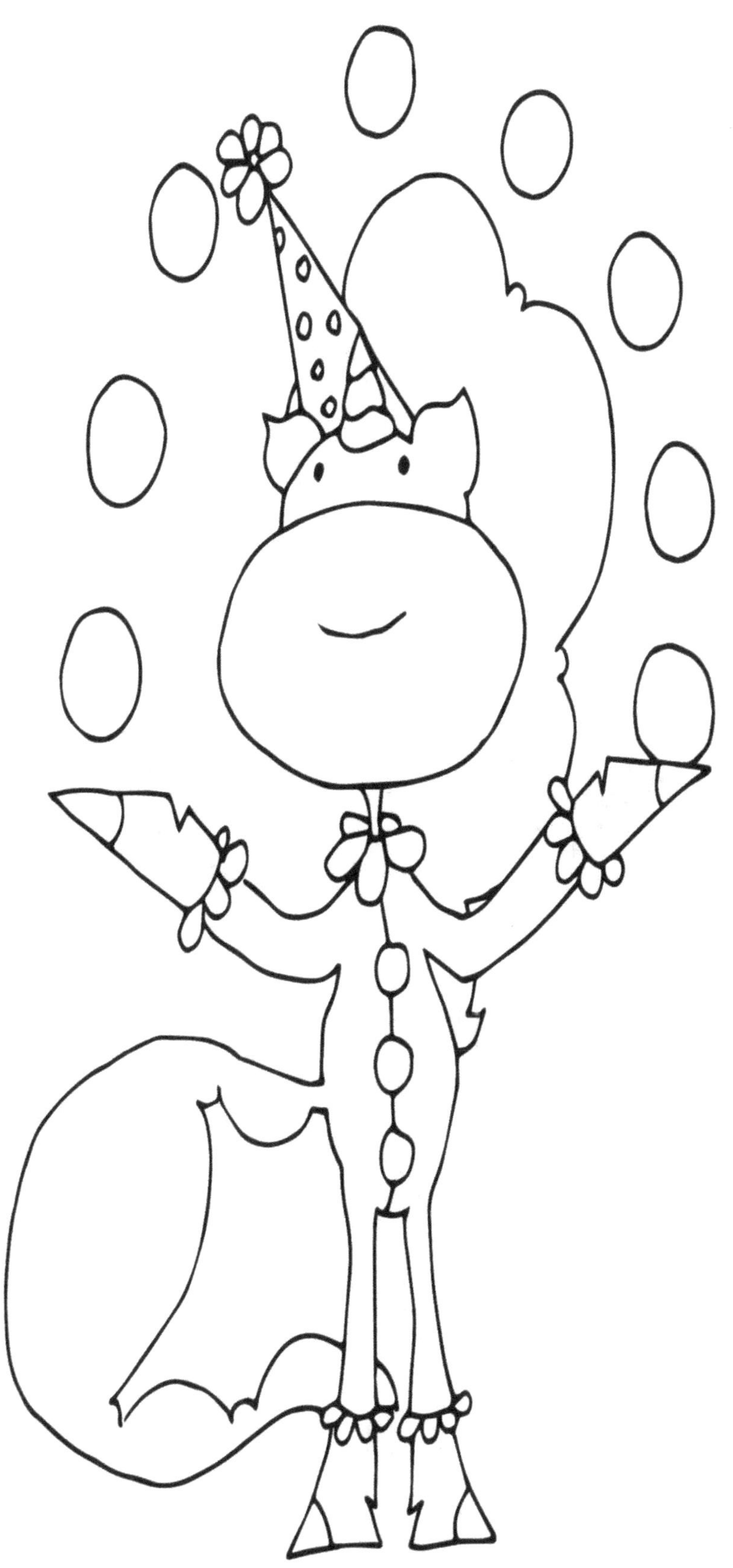

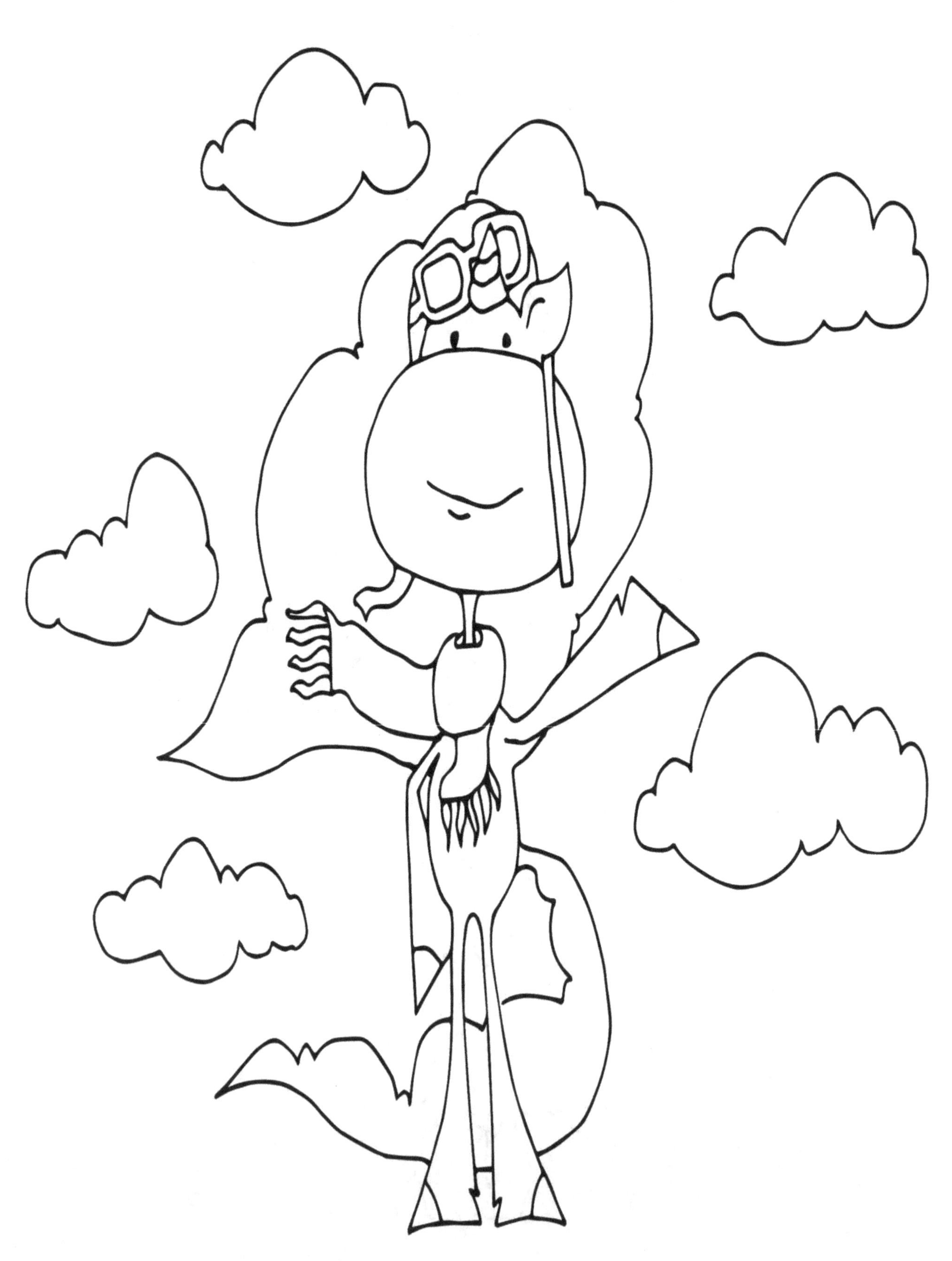

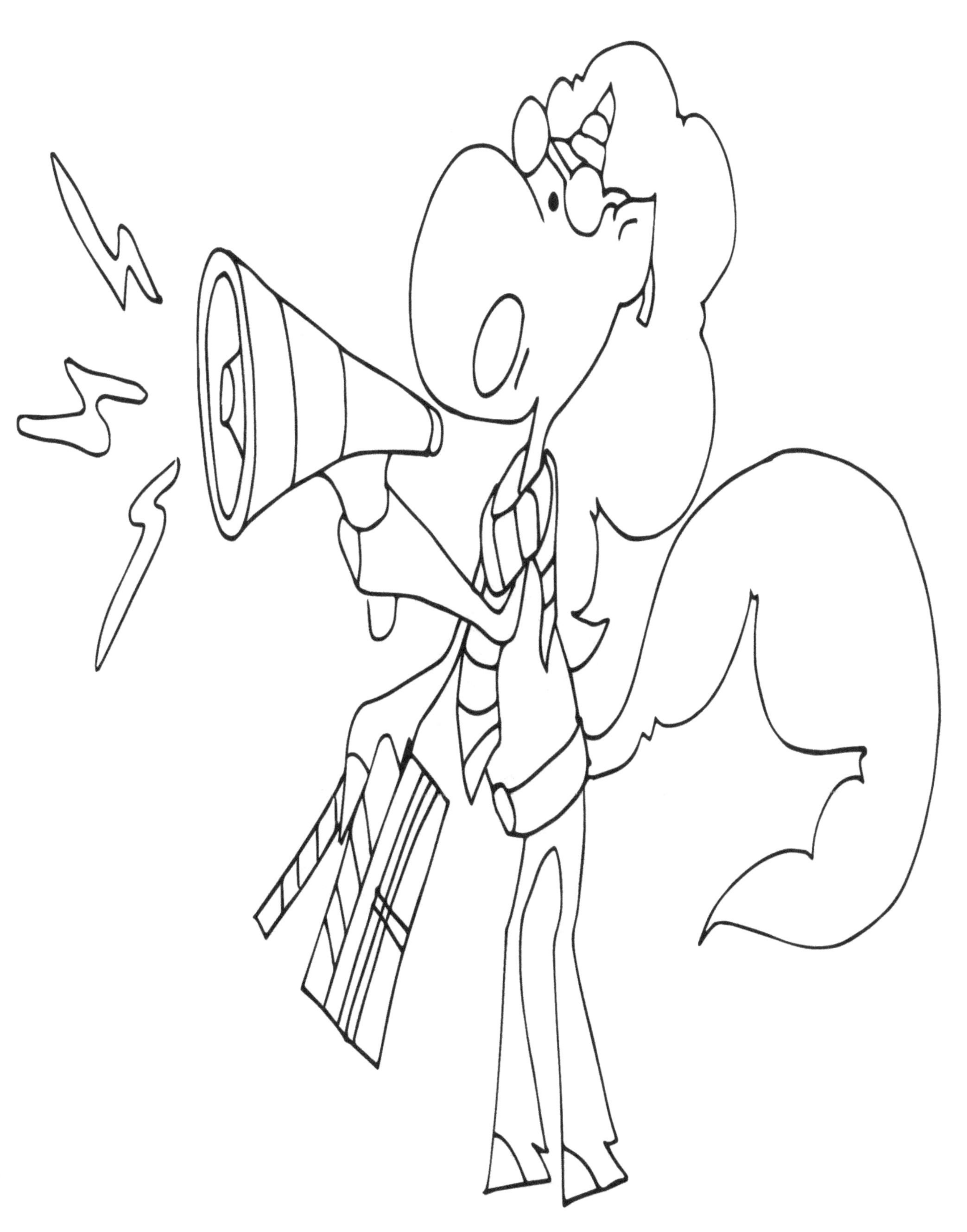

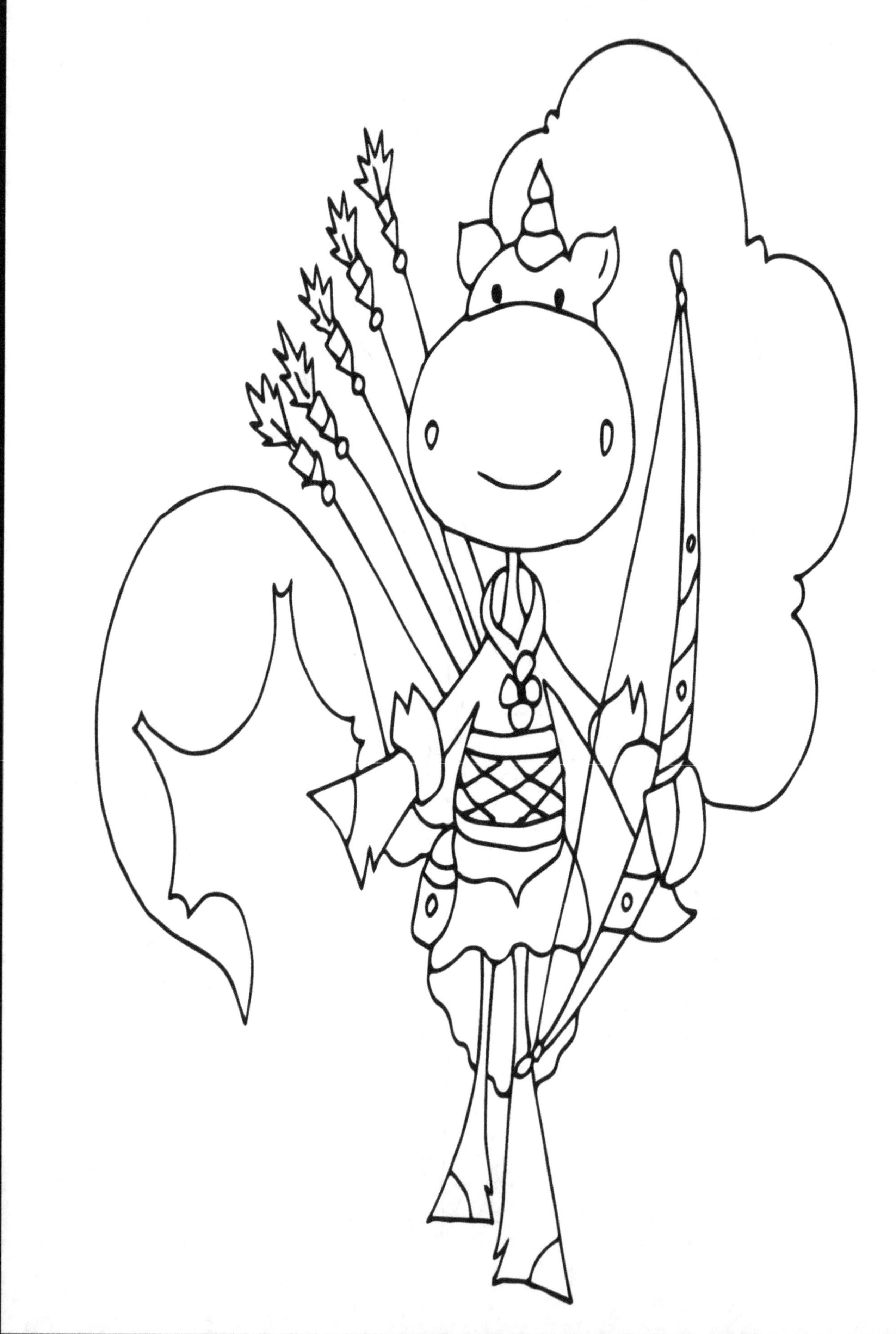

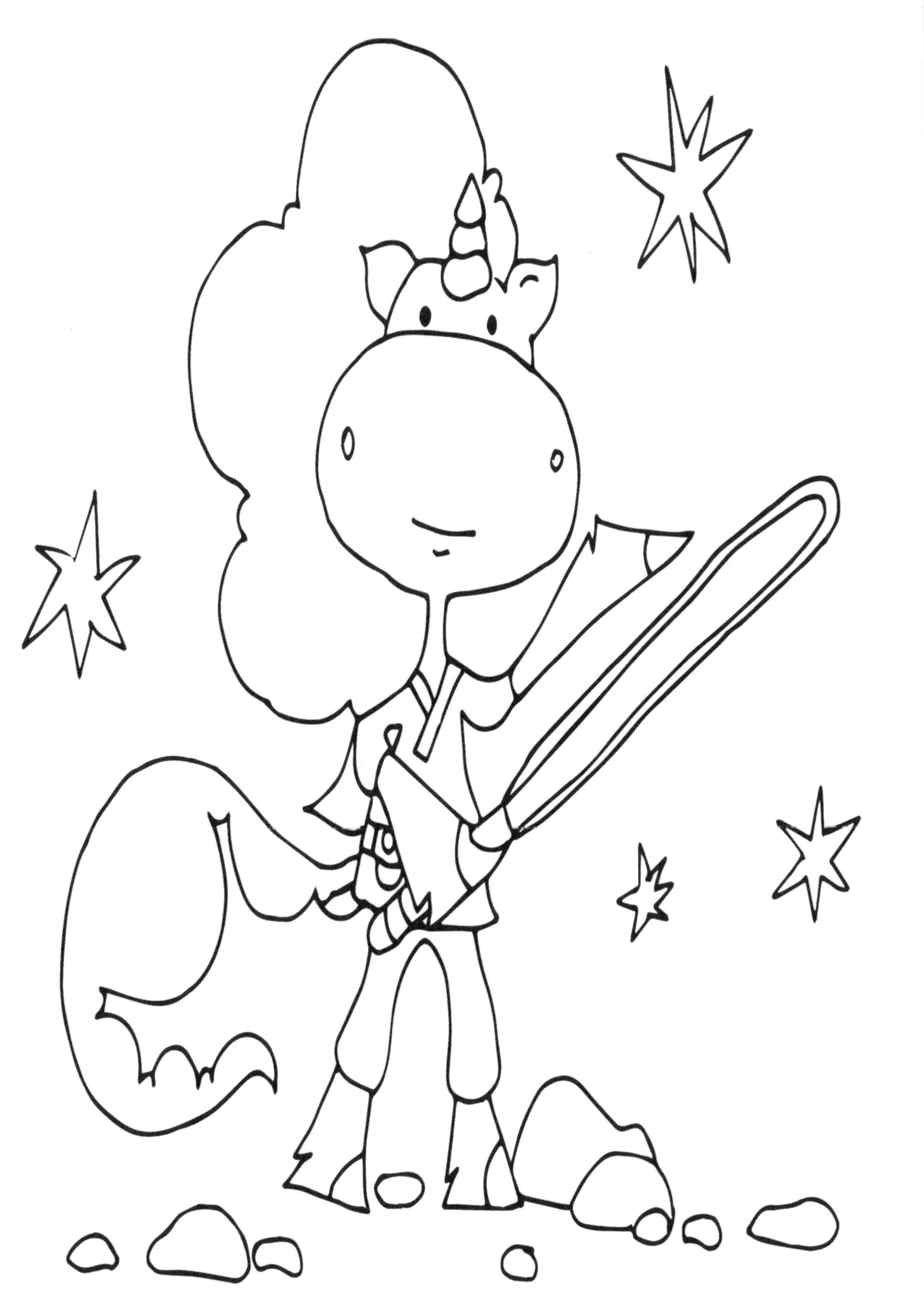

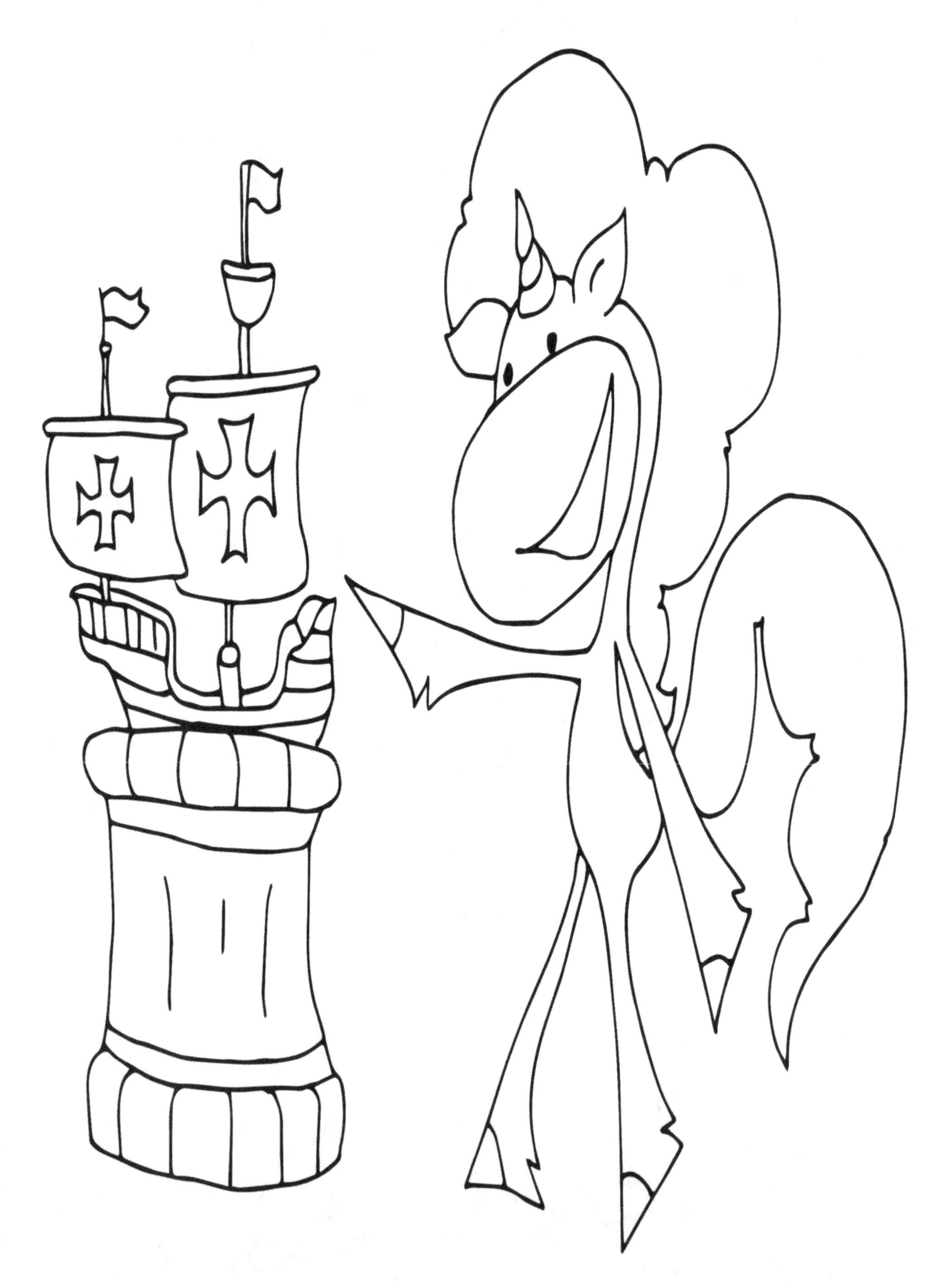

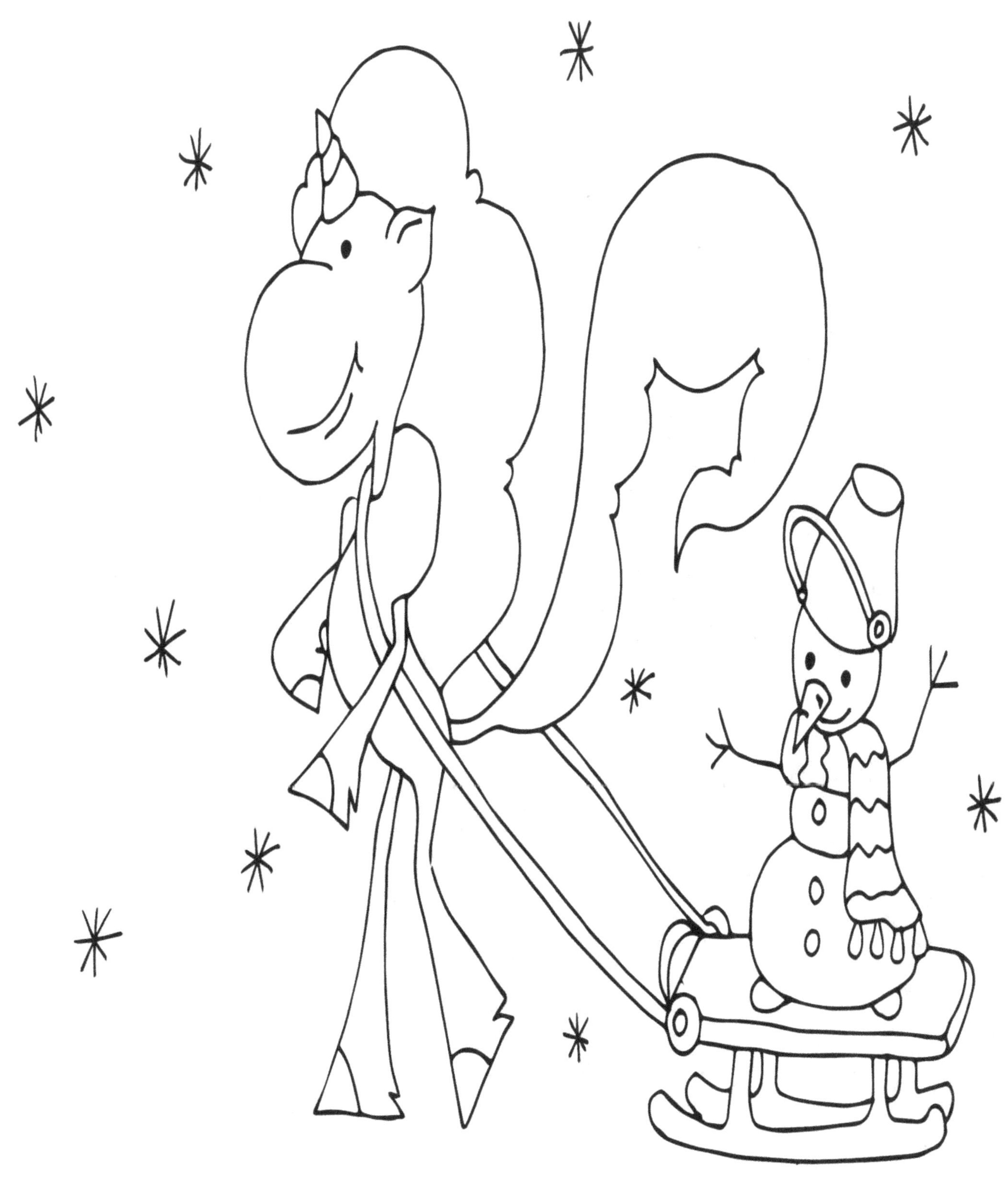

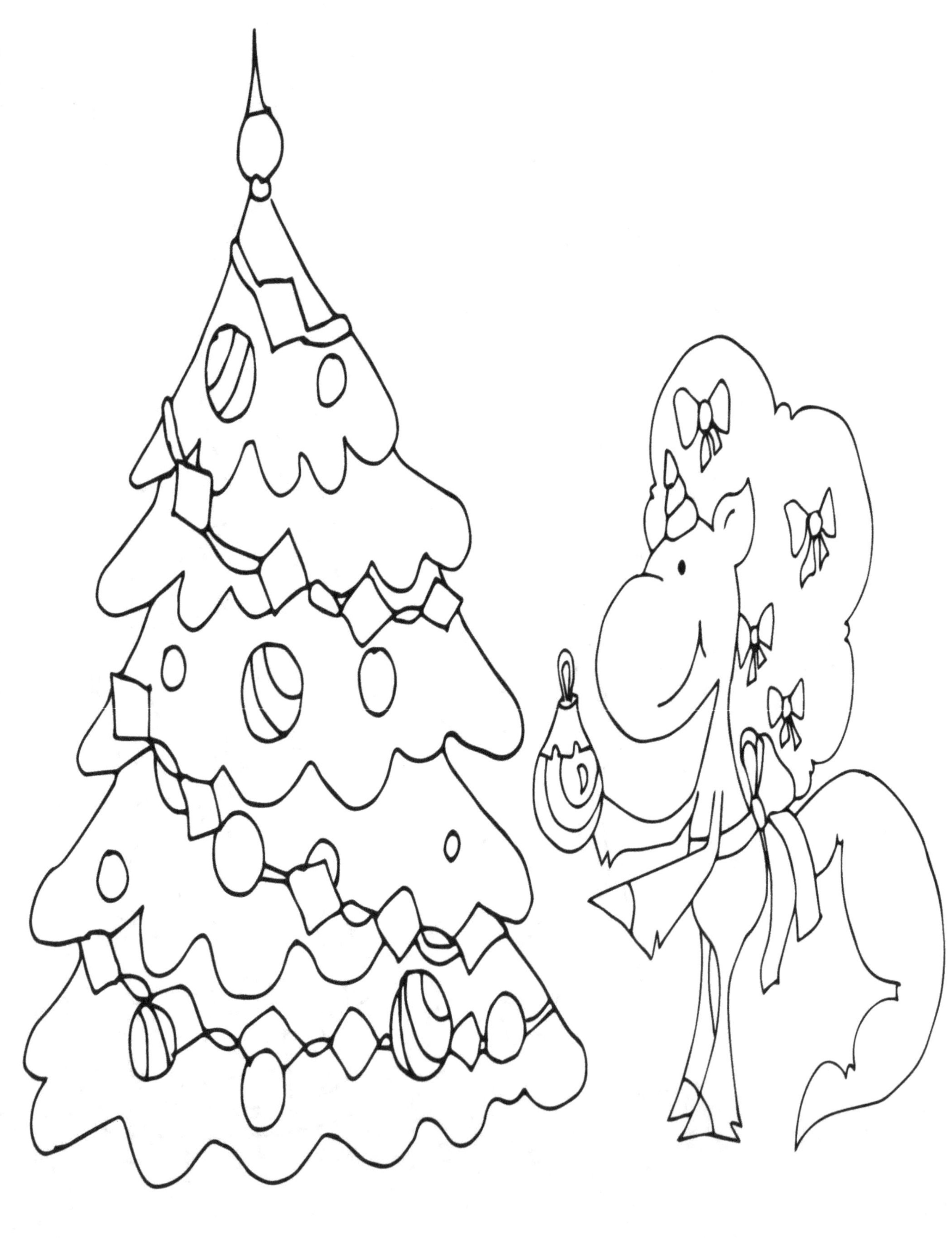

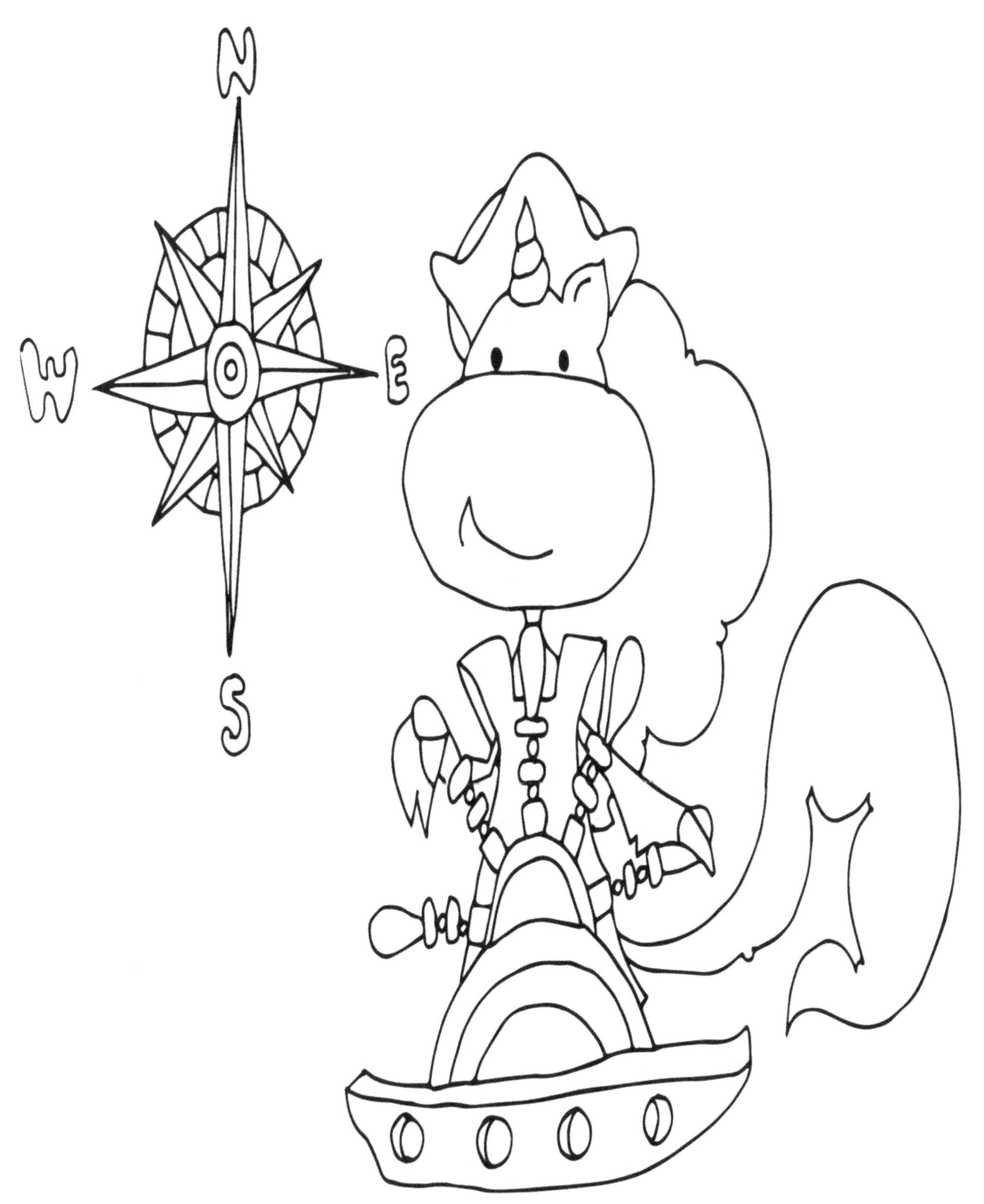

N
W
E
S

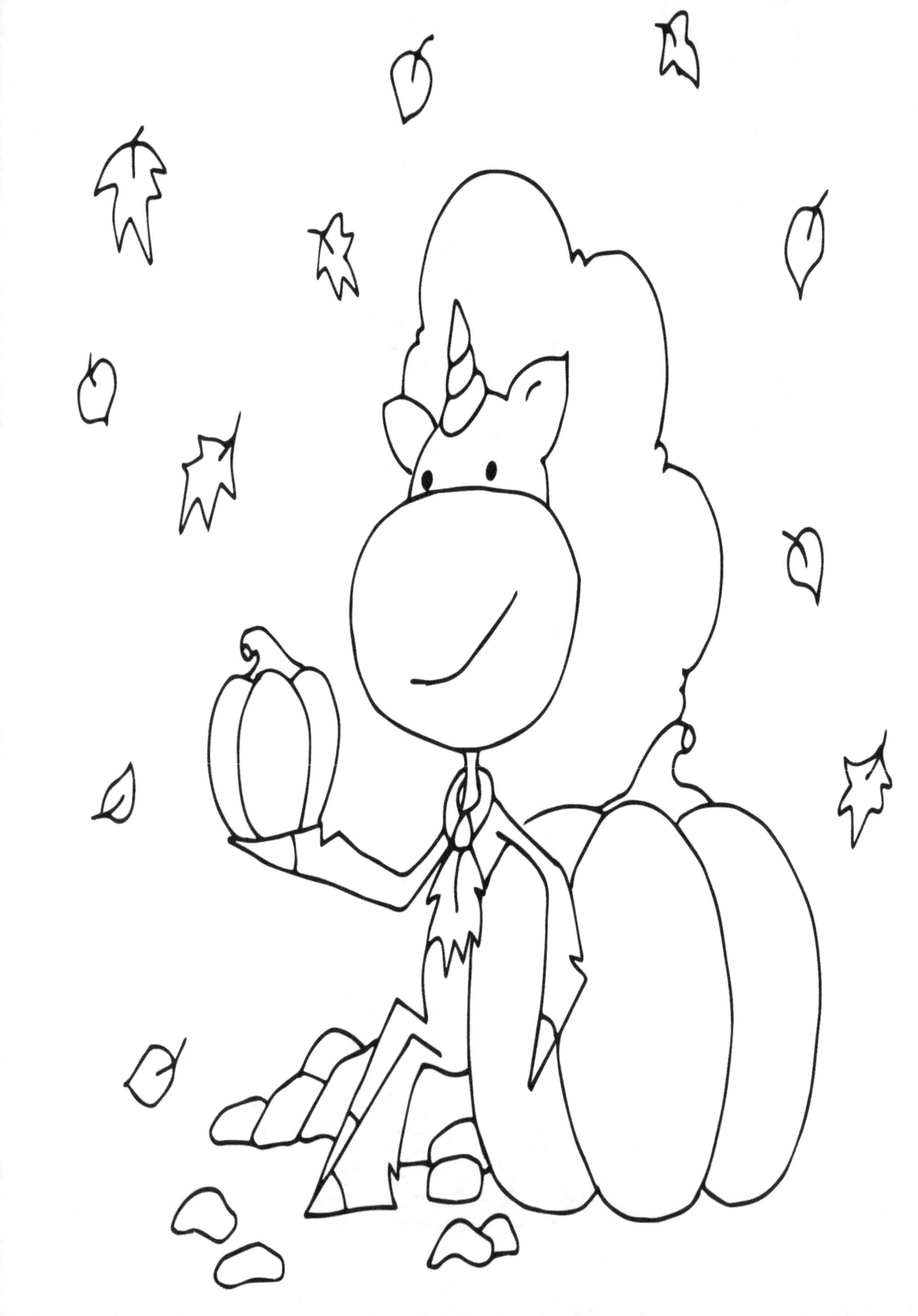

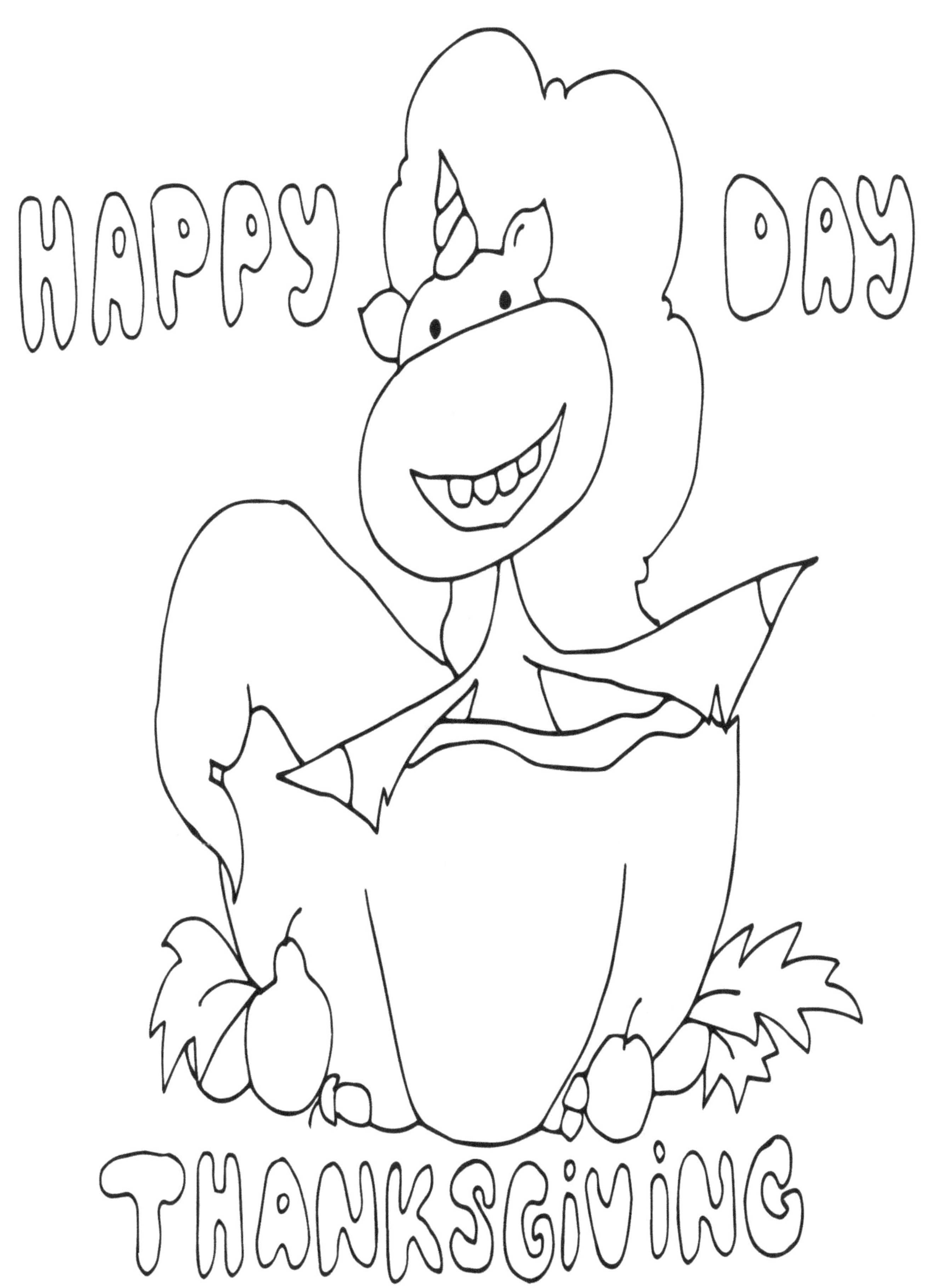

HAPPY
DAY
THANKSGIVING

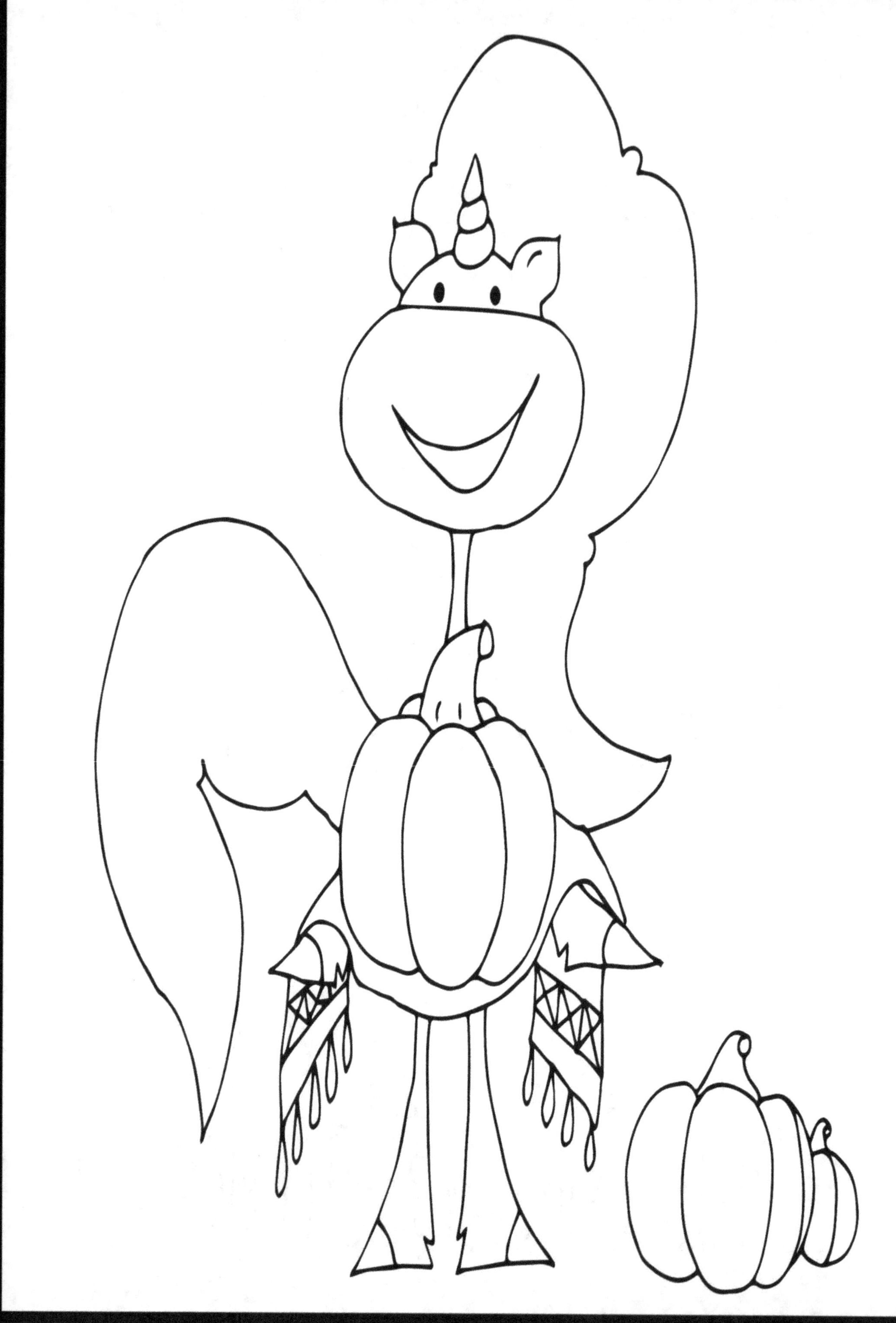

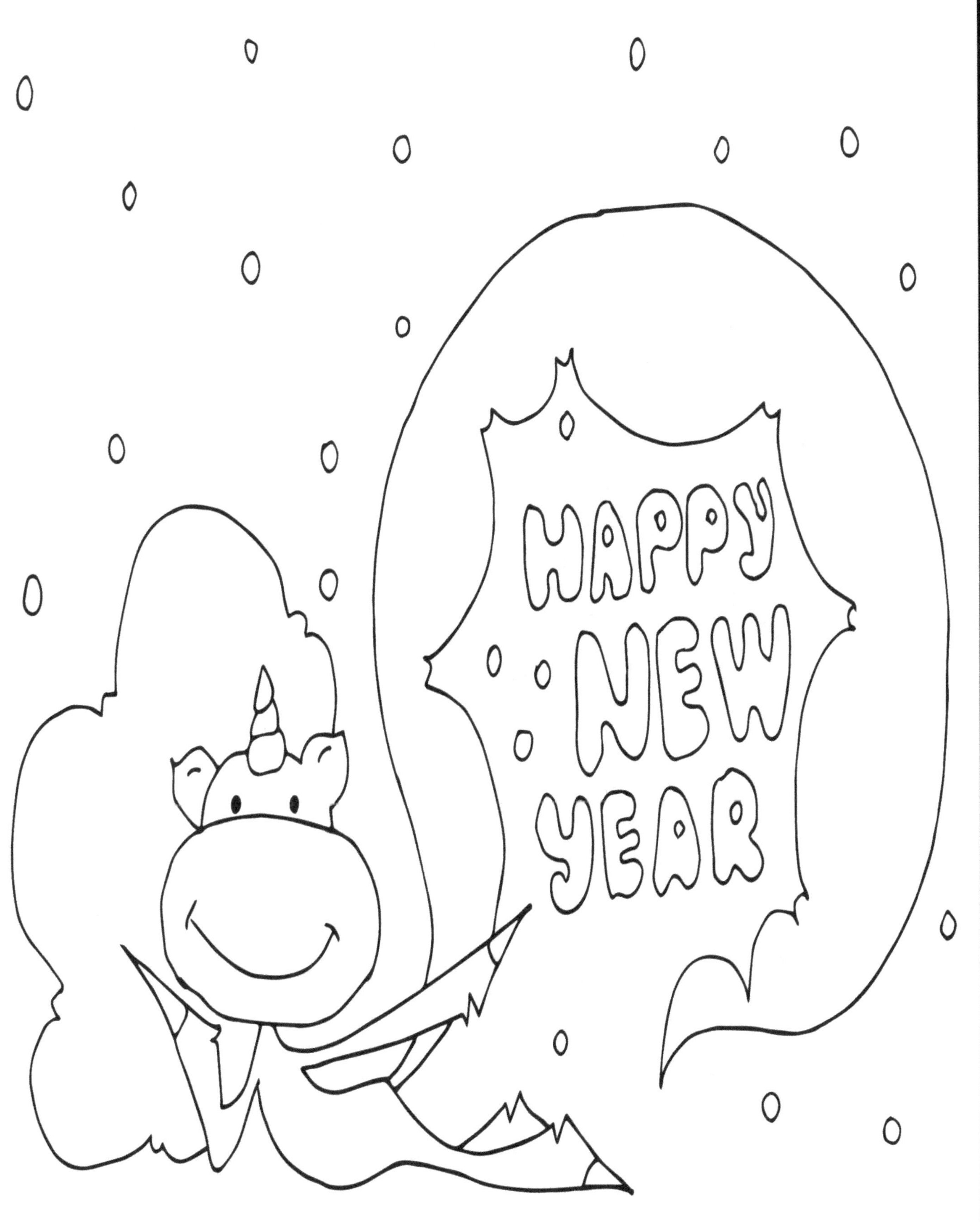

HAPPY
NEW
YEAR

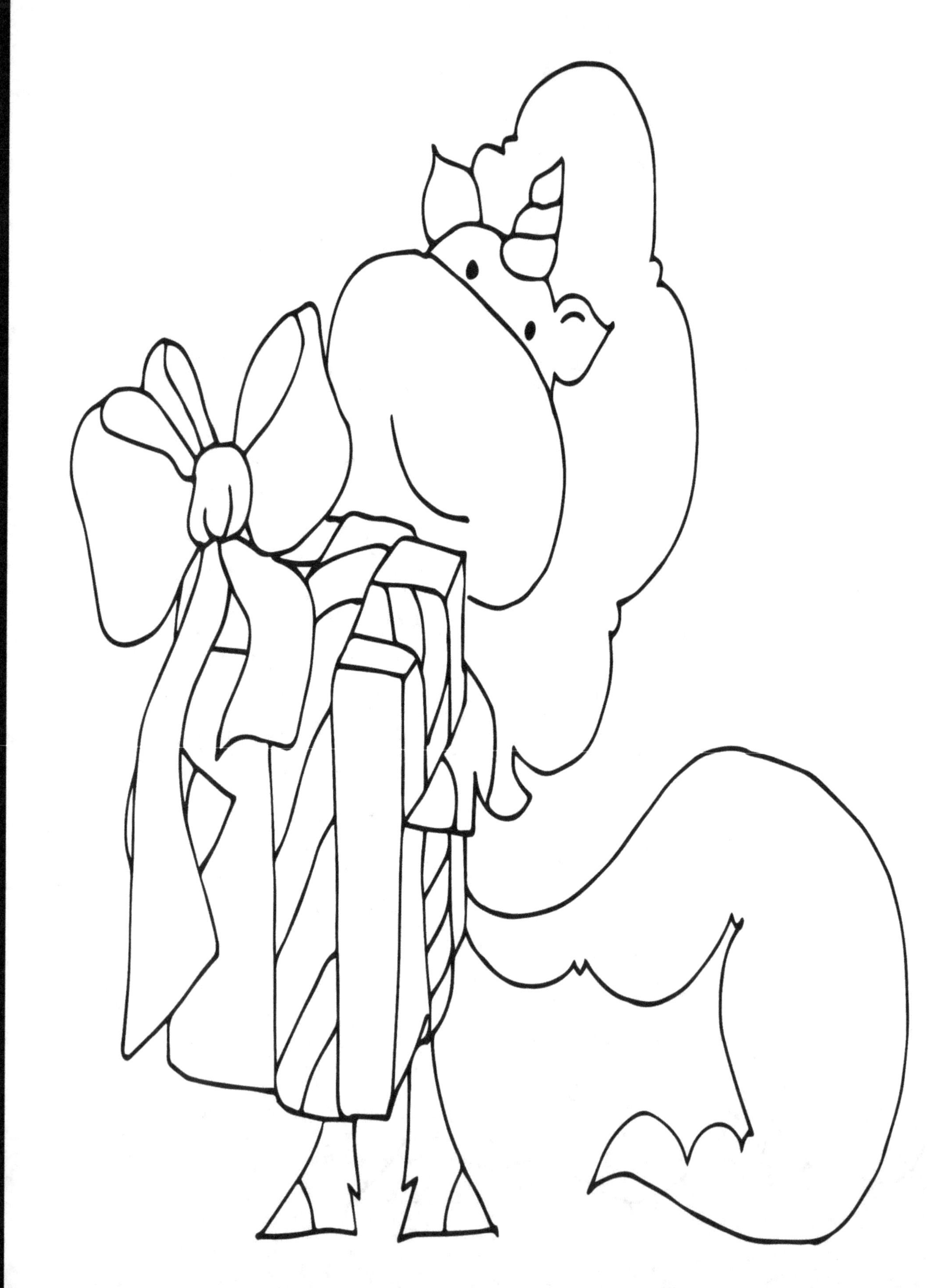

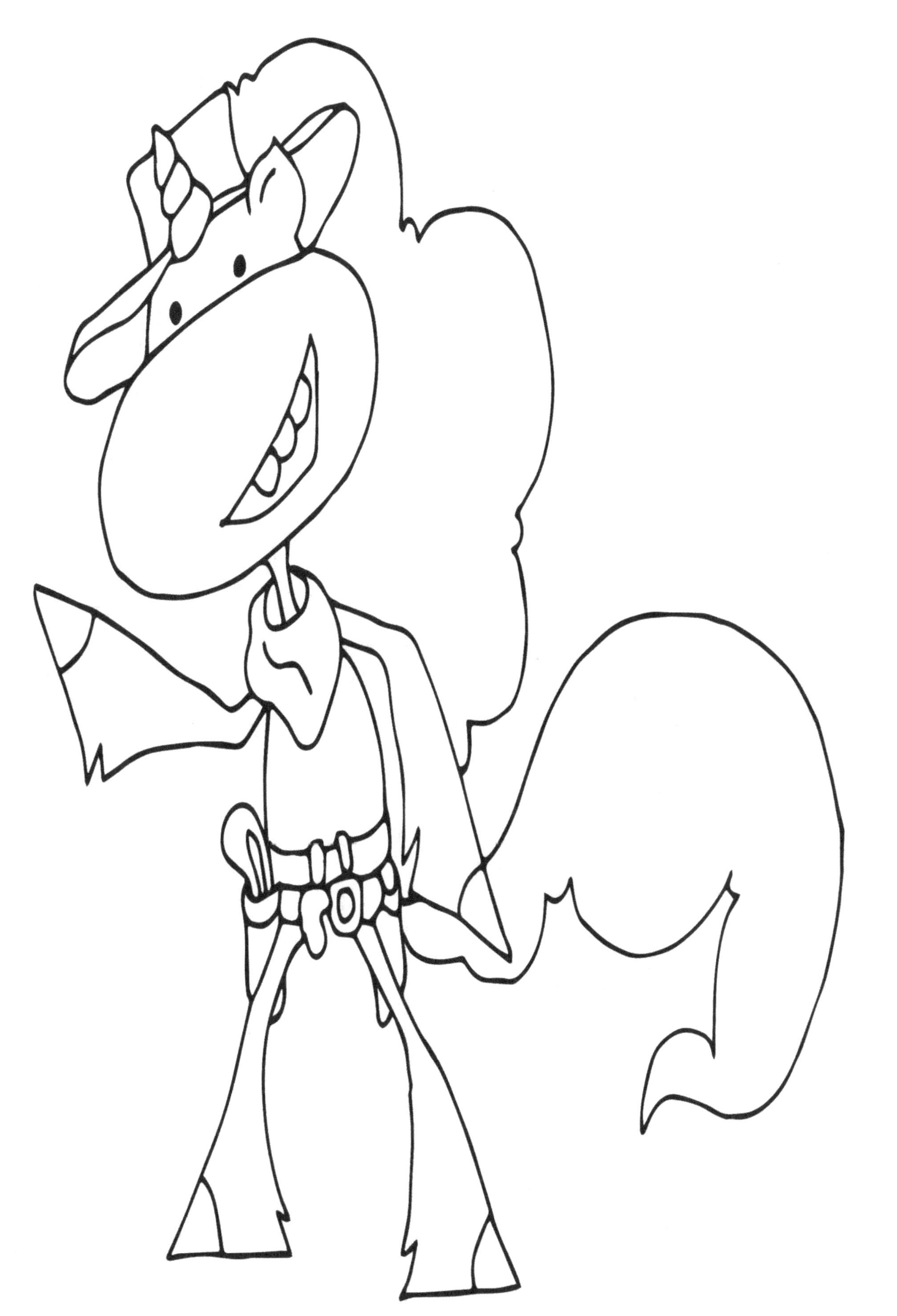

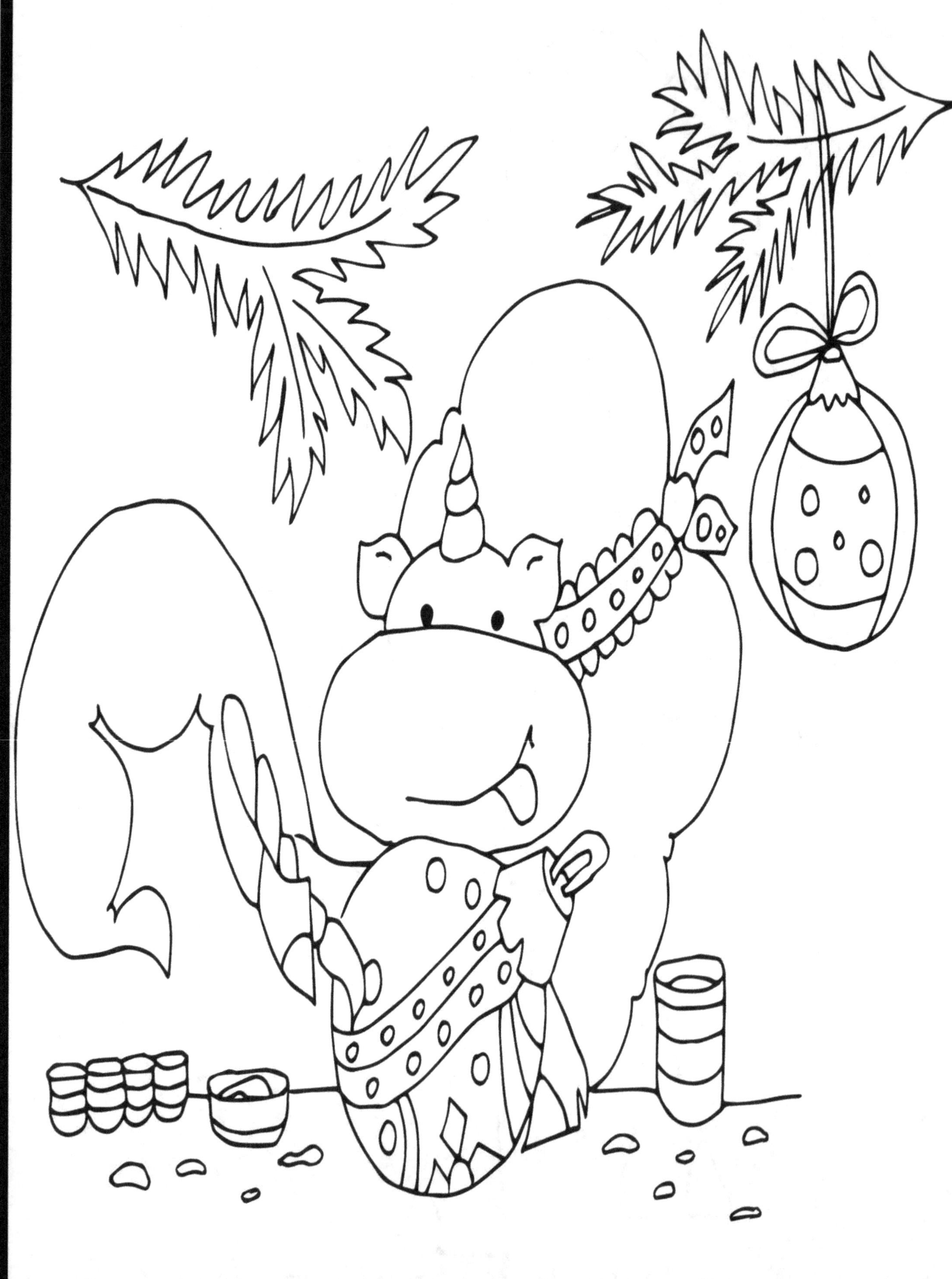

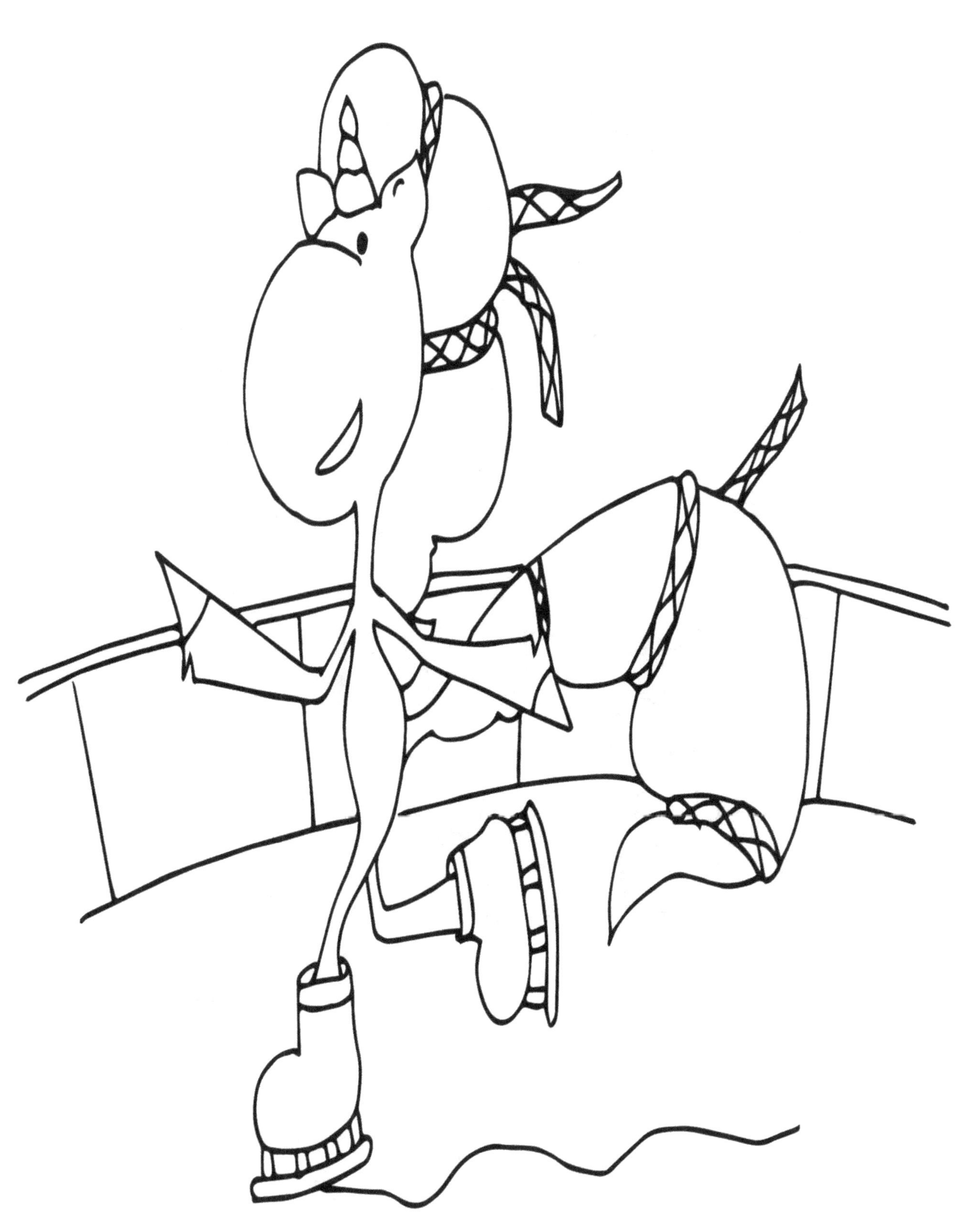

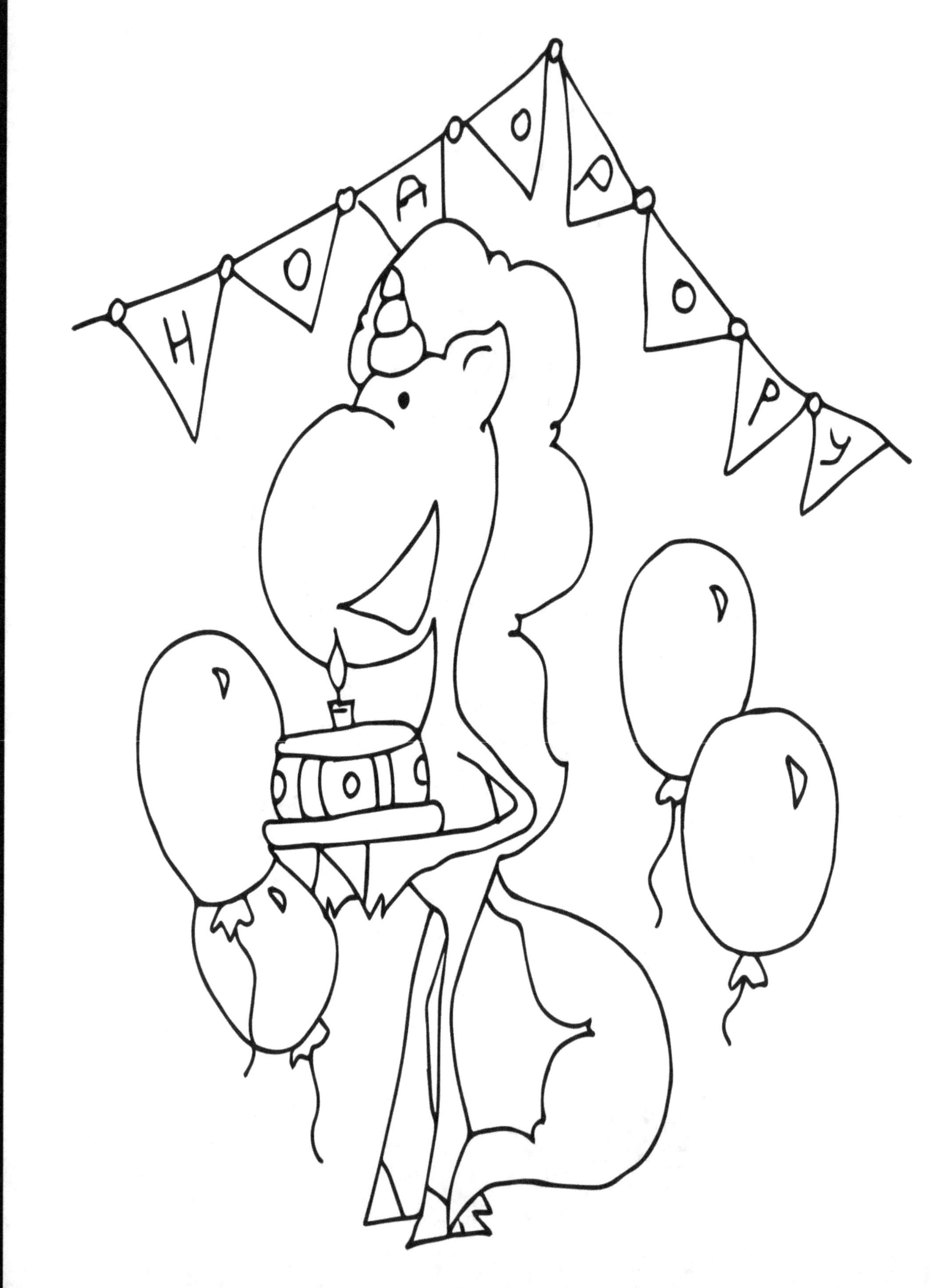

H
O
A
P
P
Y

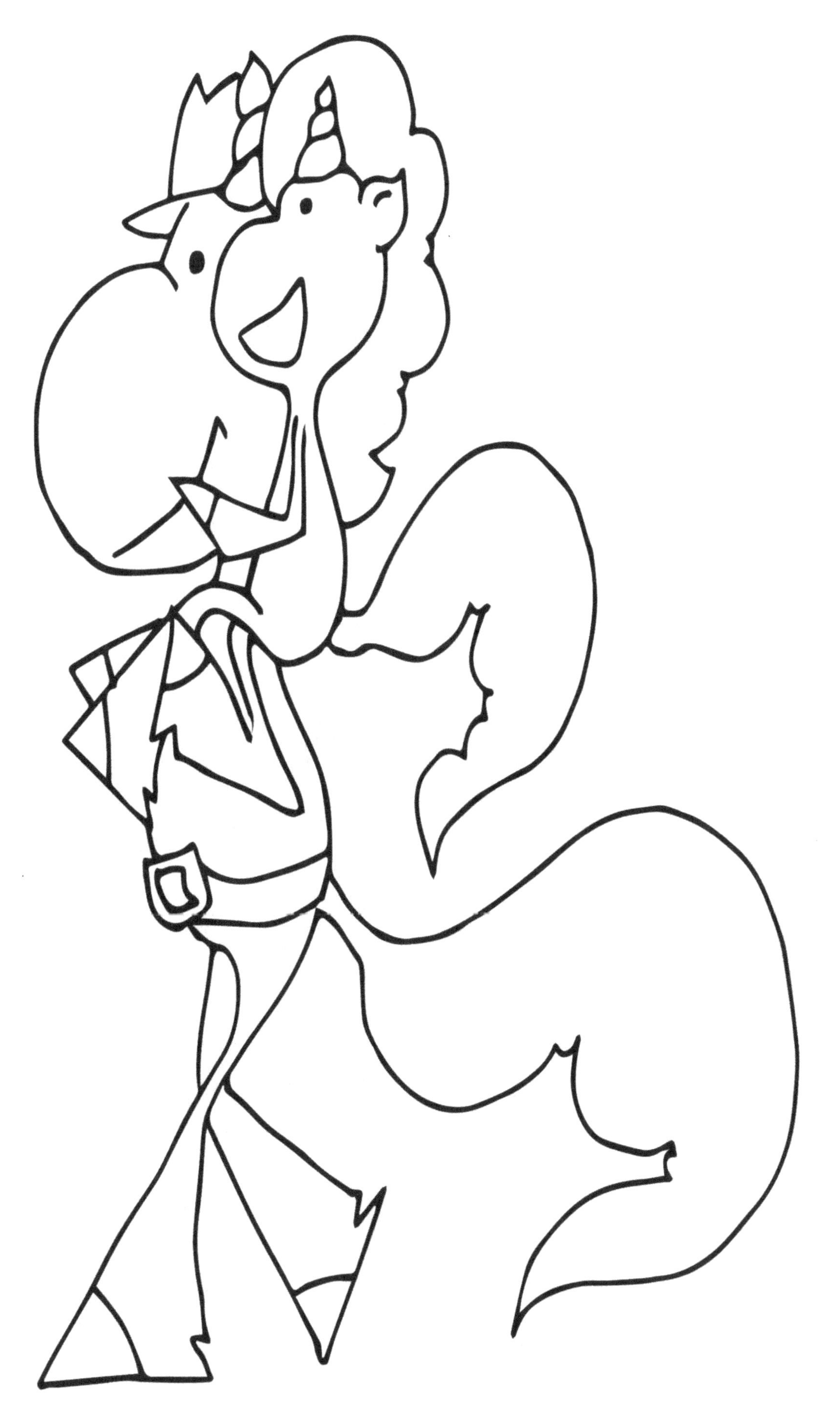

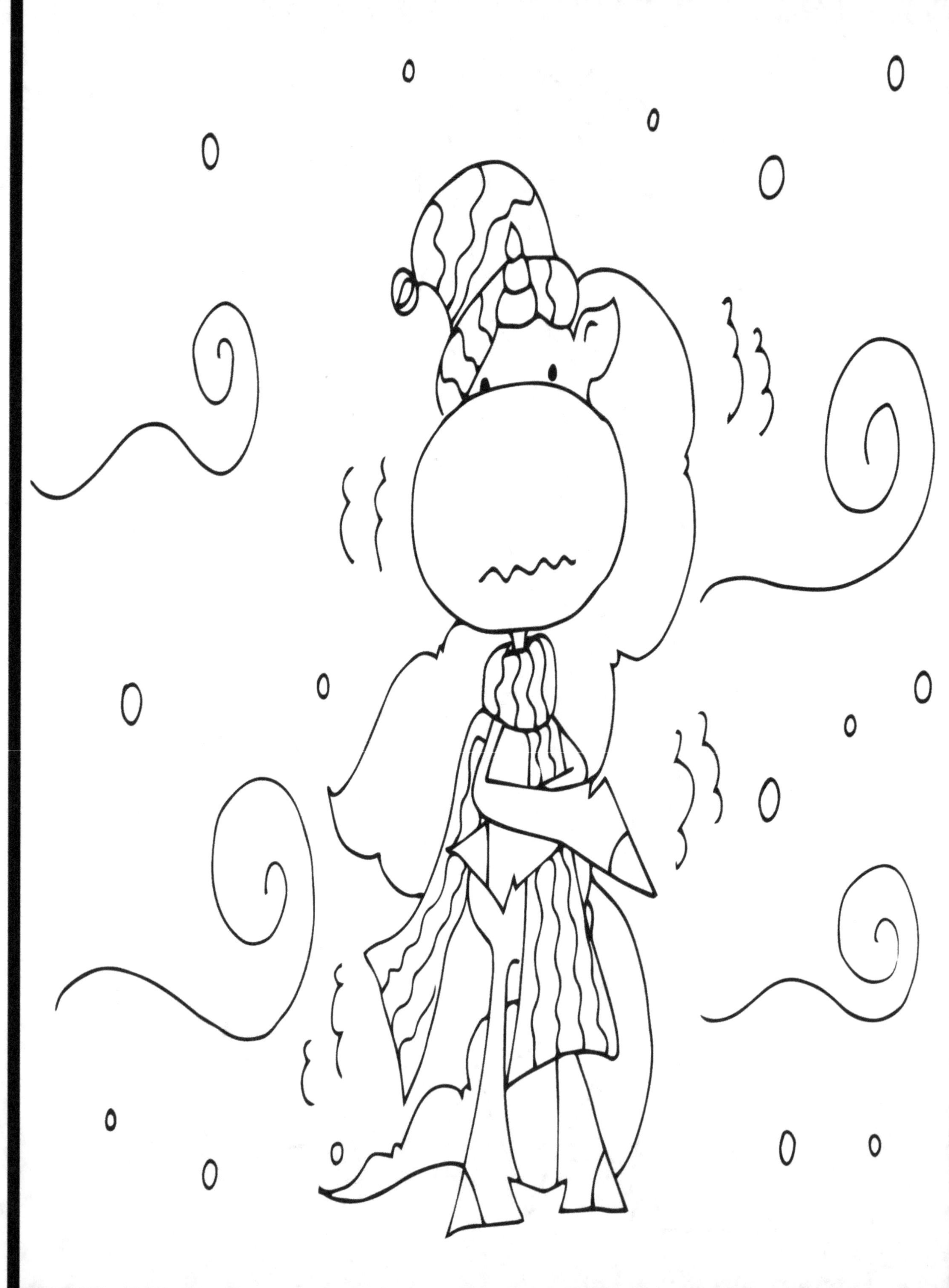

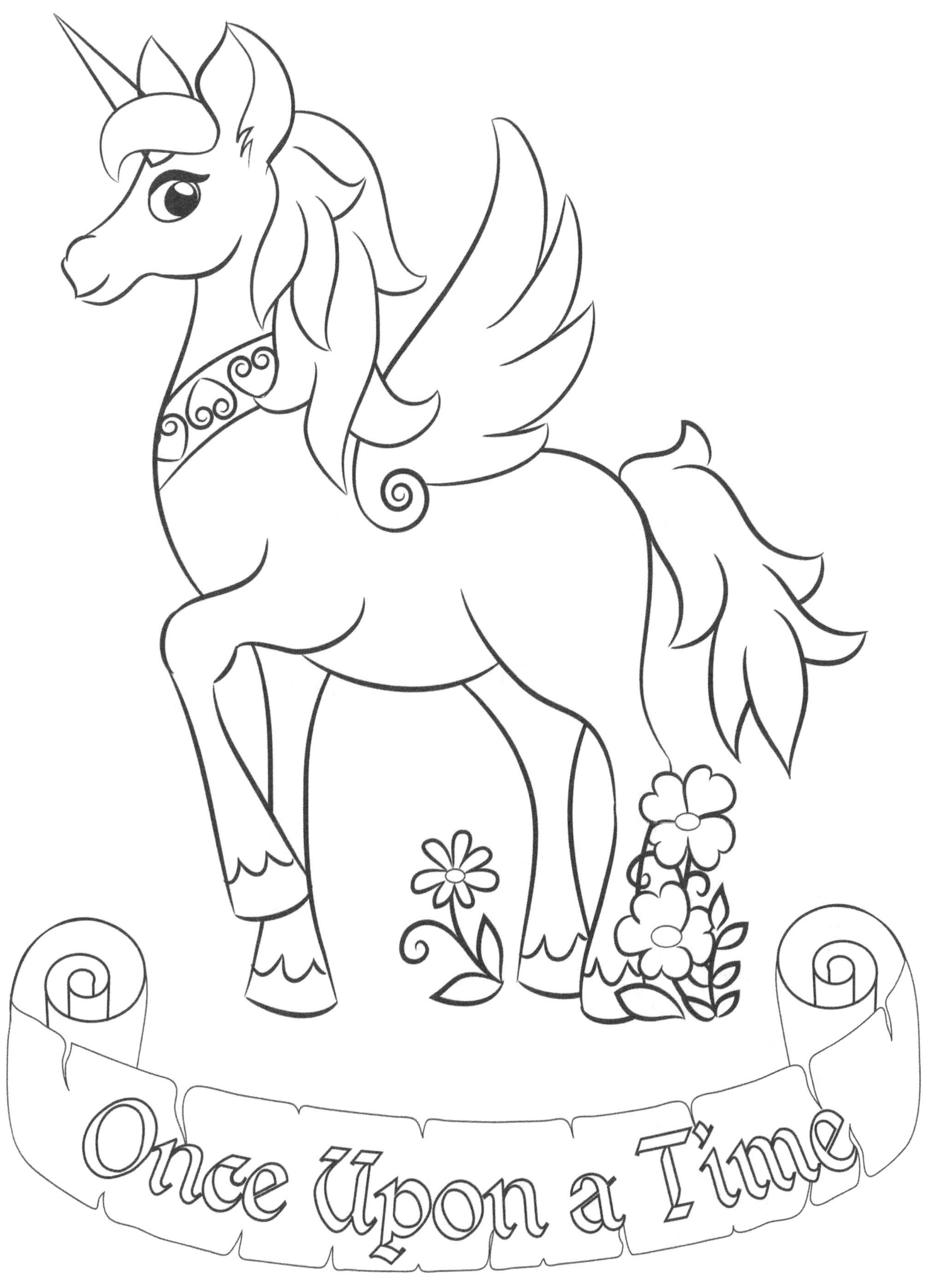

Once Upon a Time

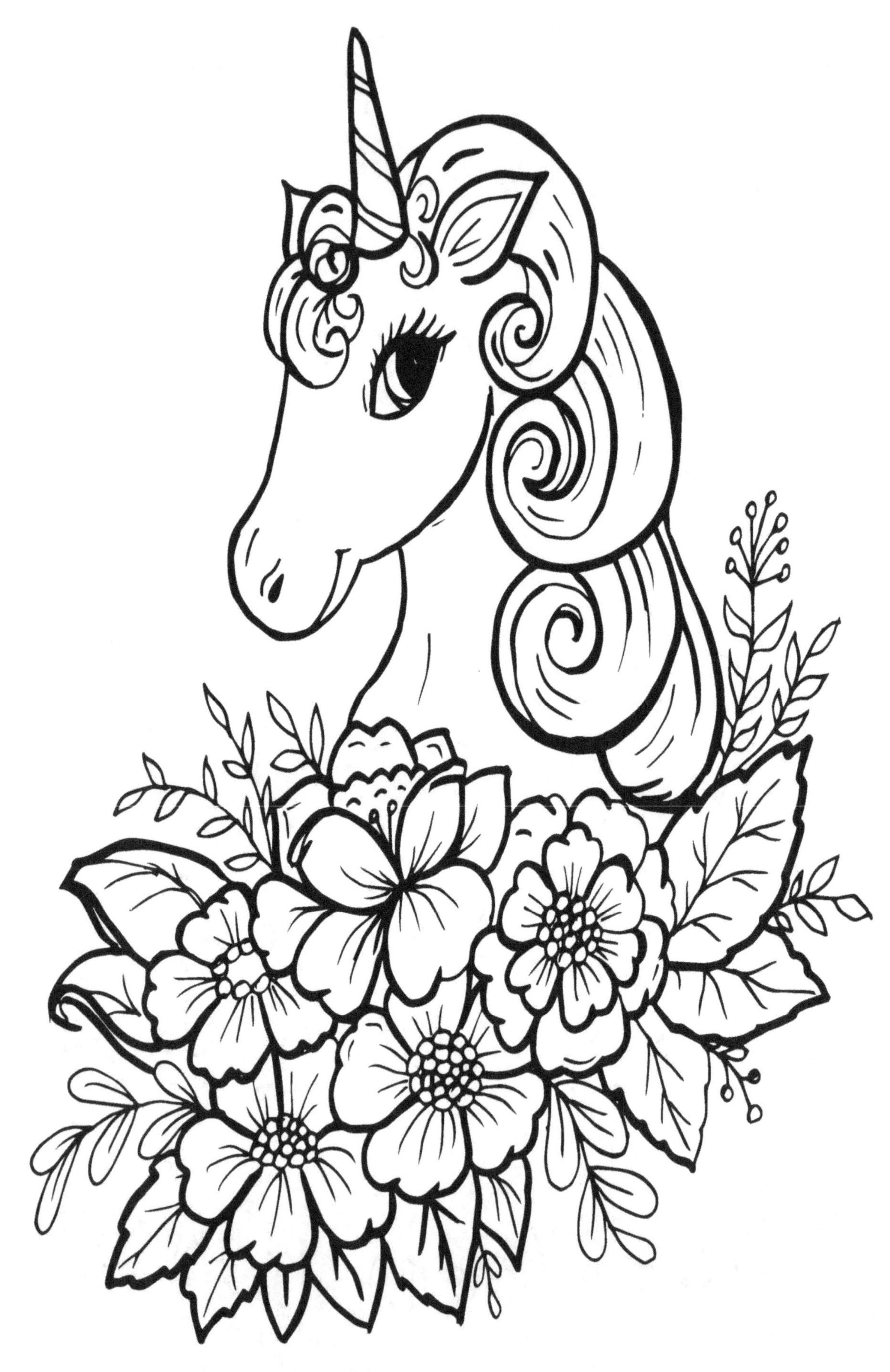

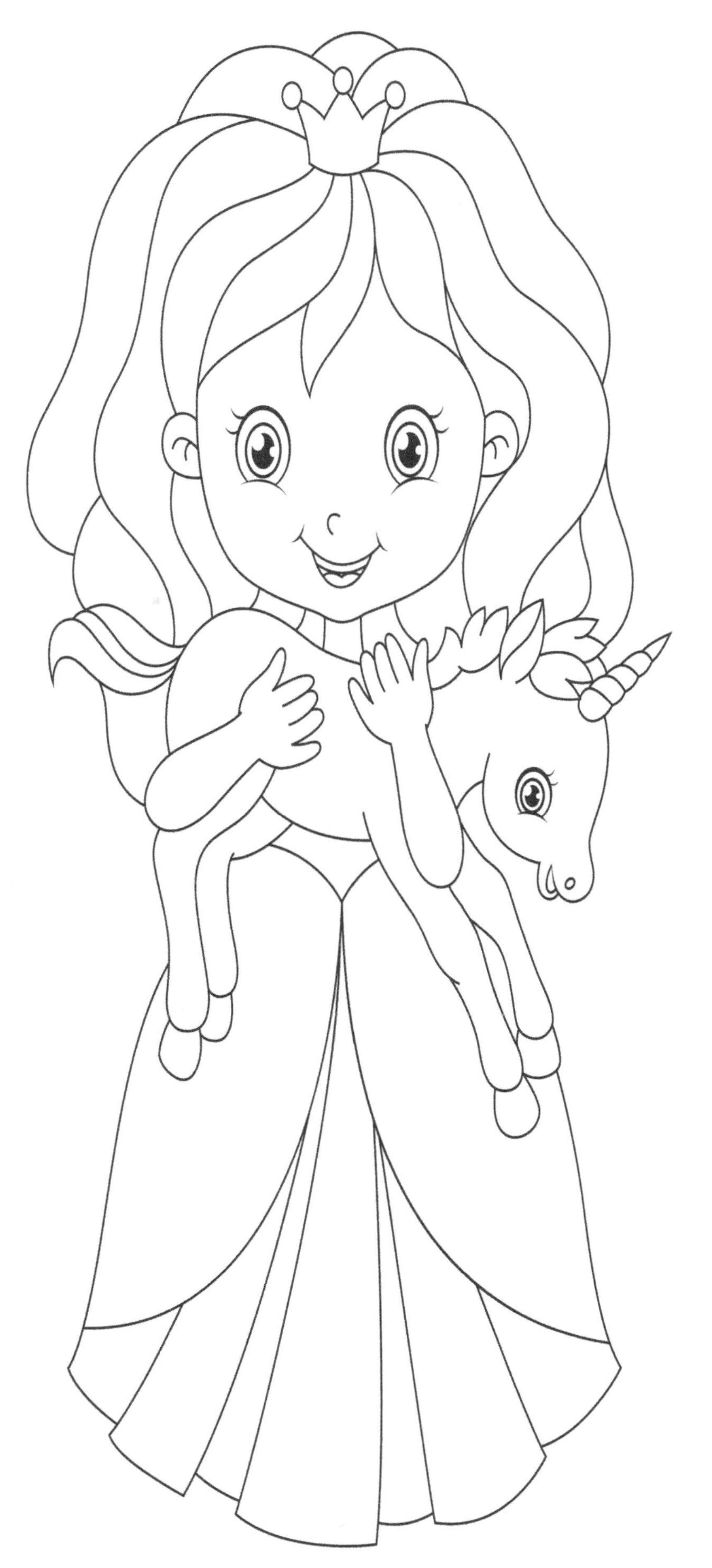

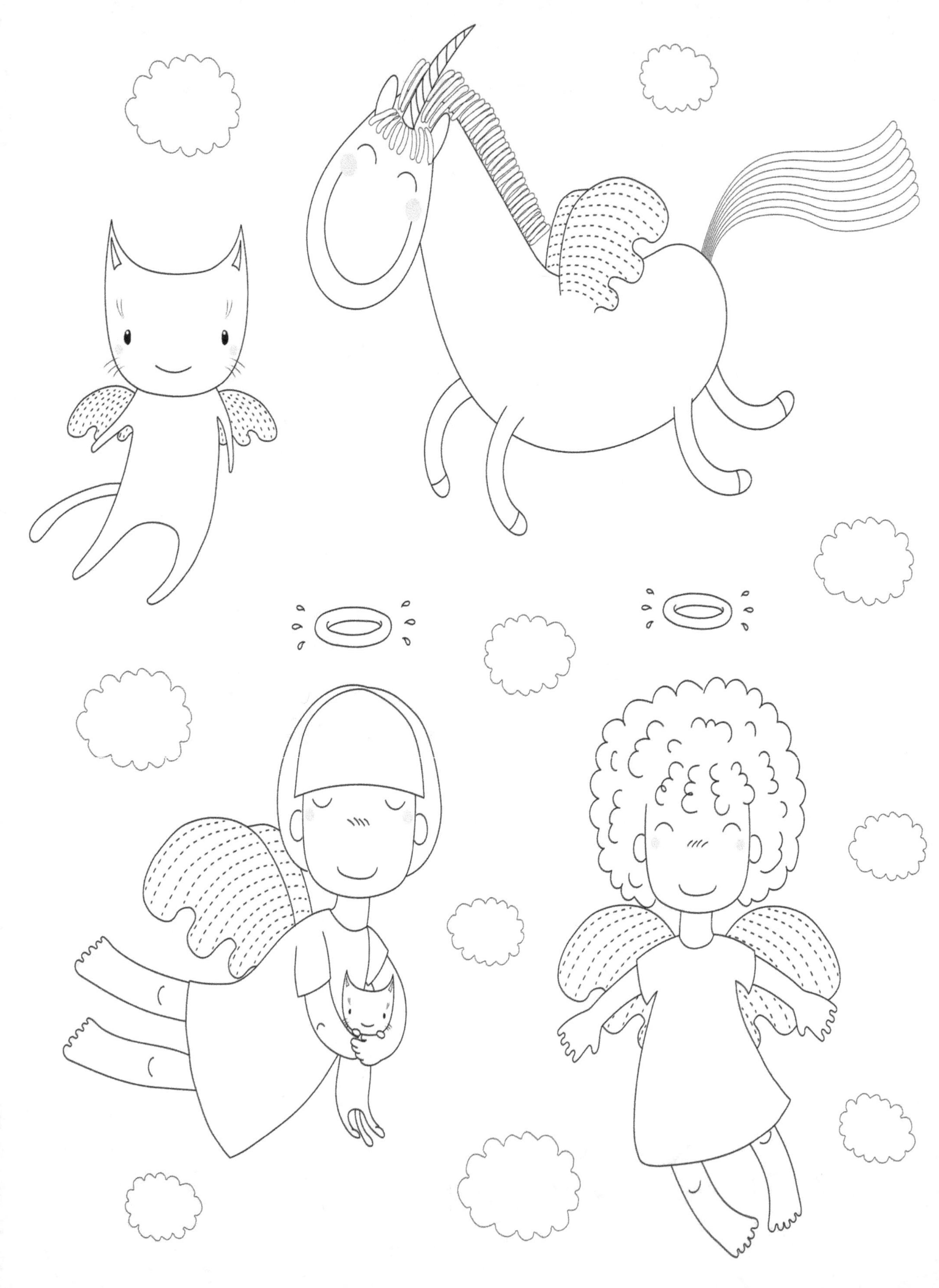

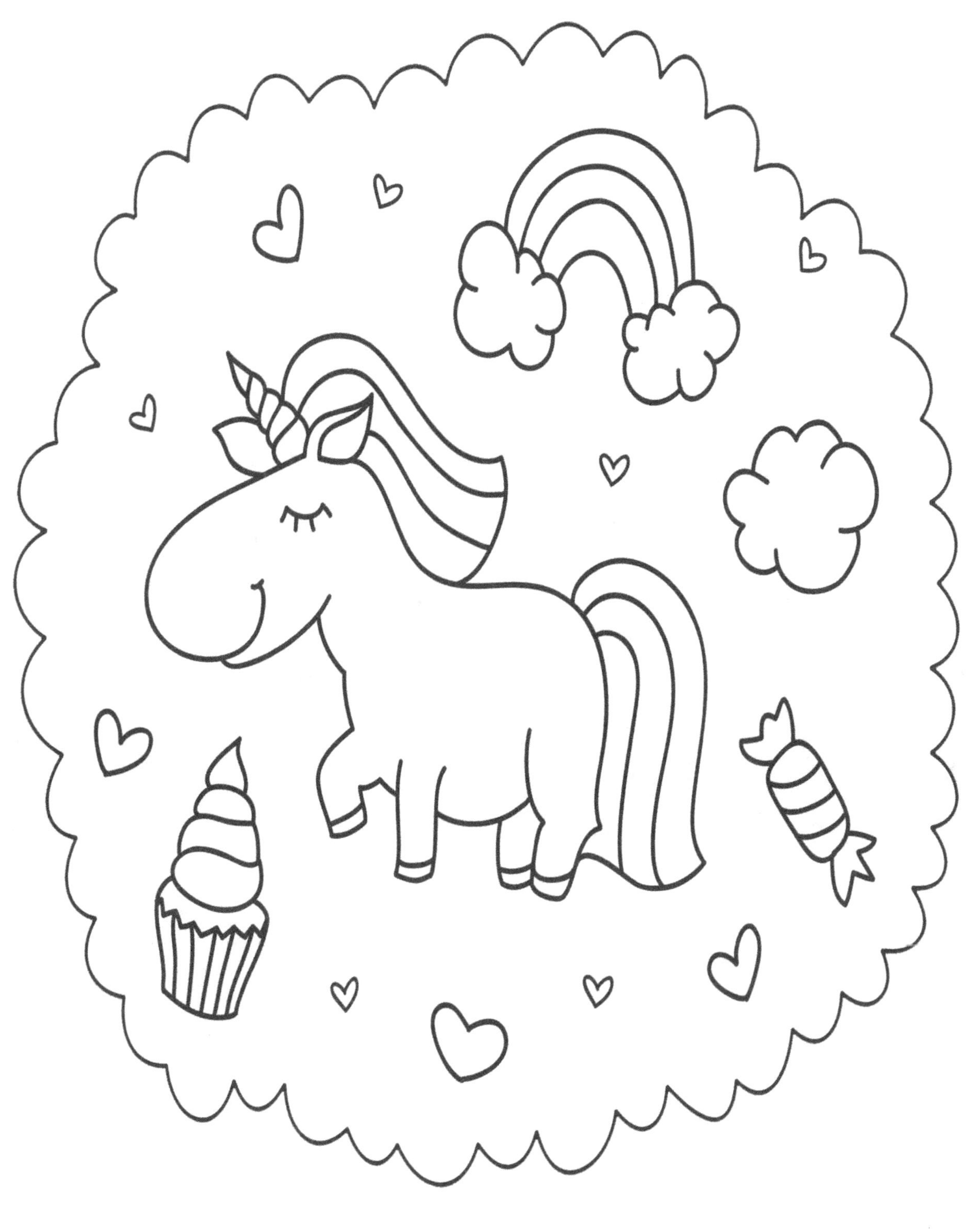

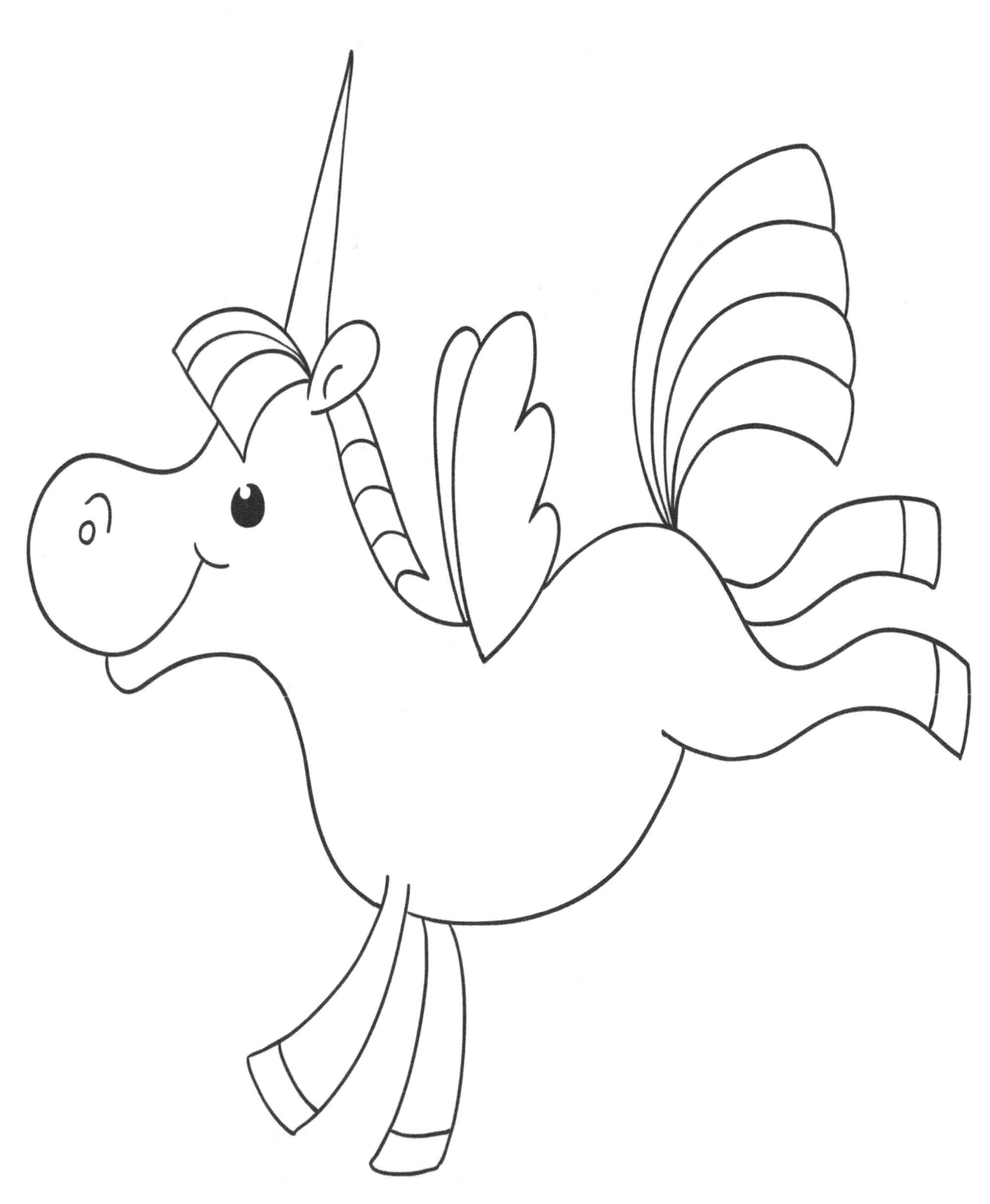

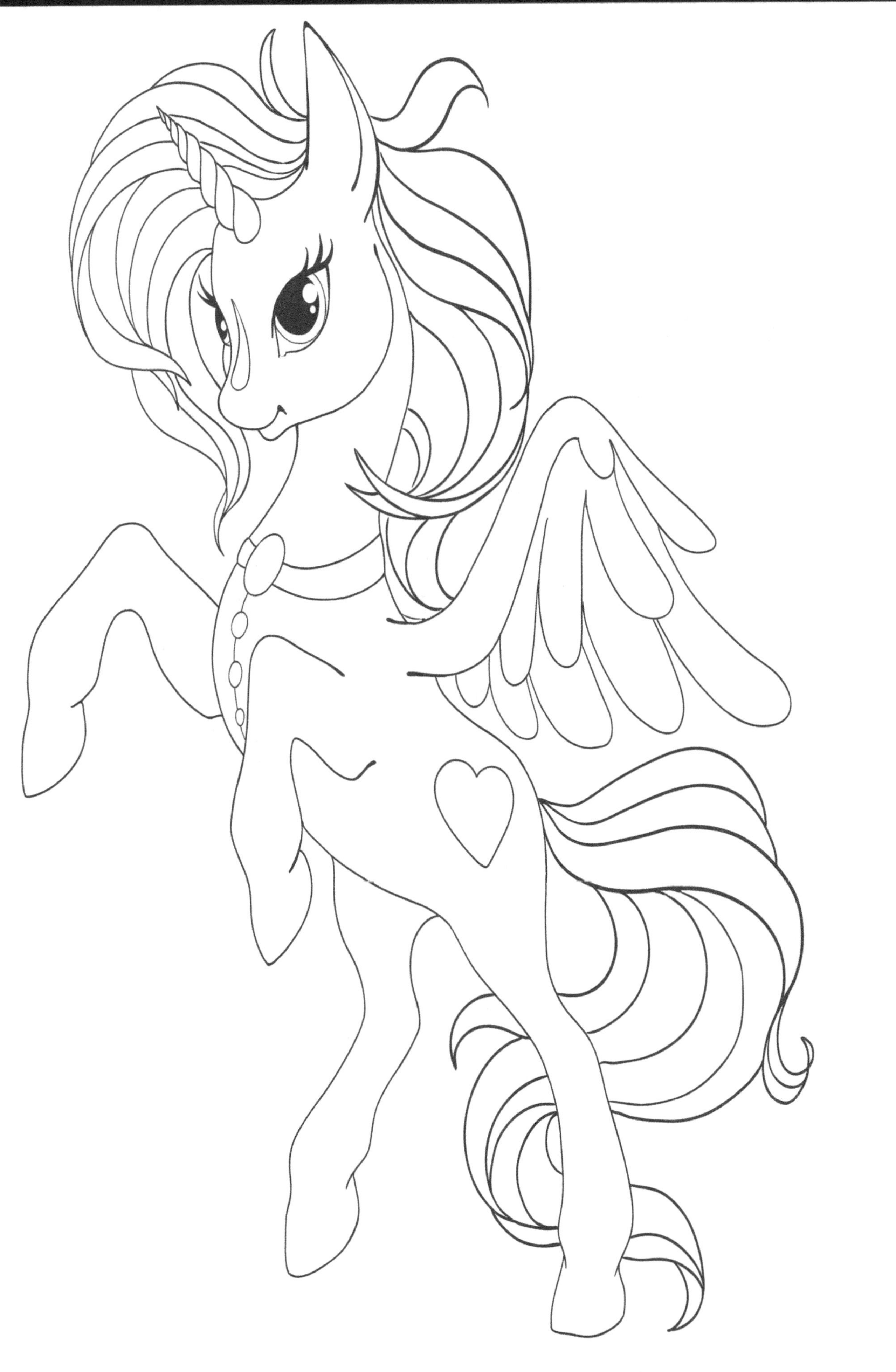

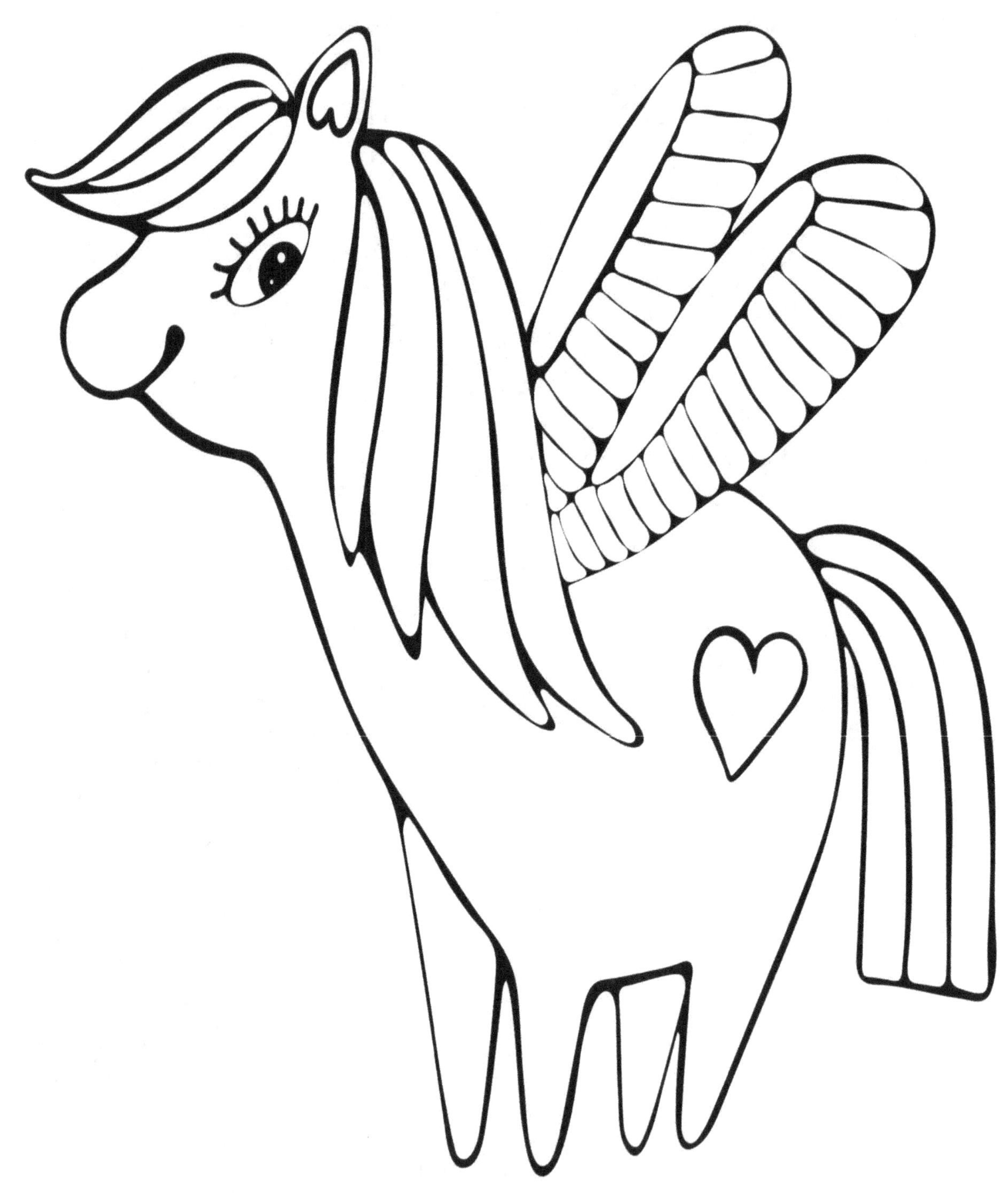

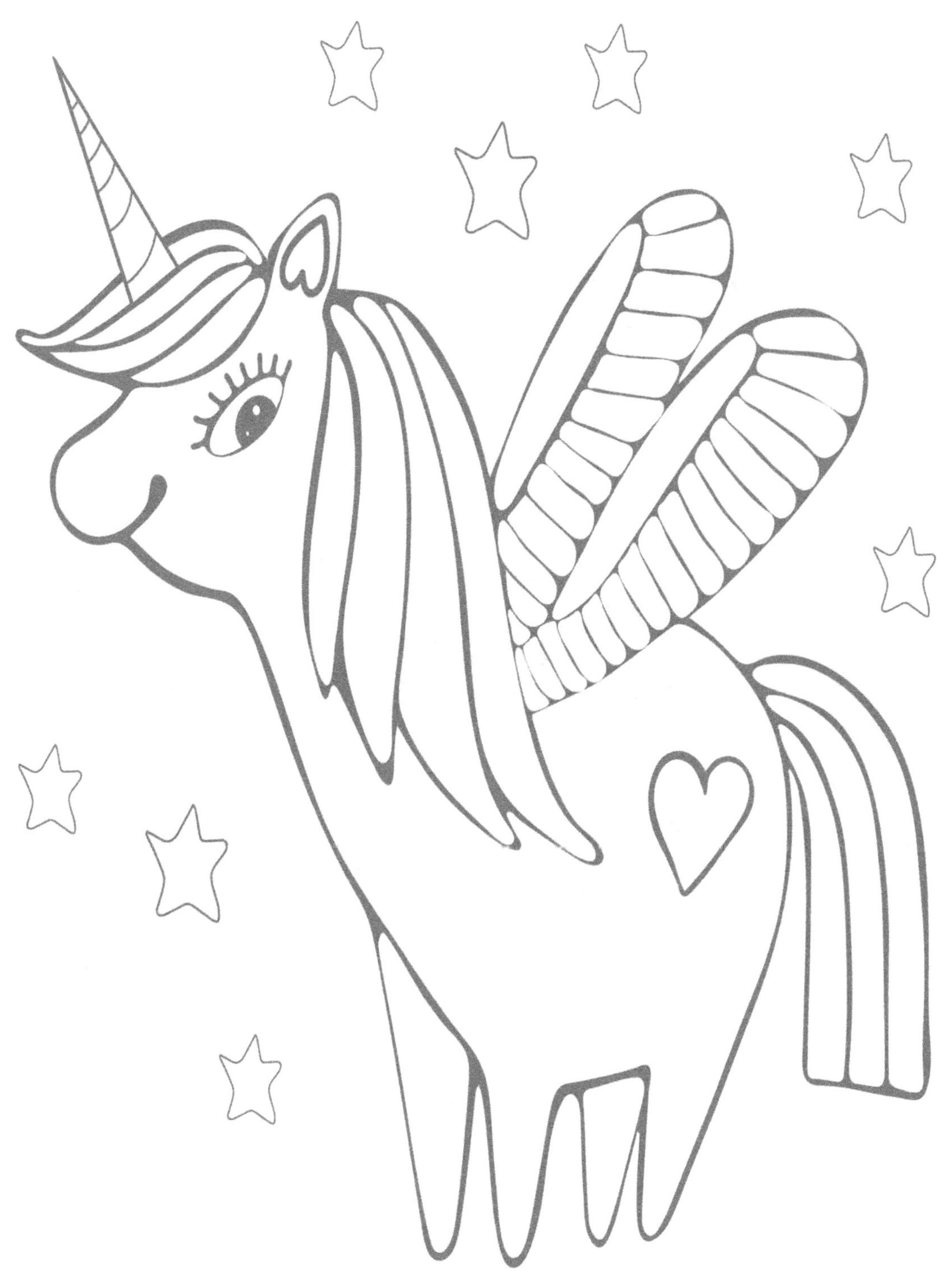

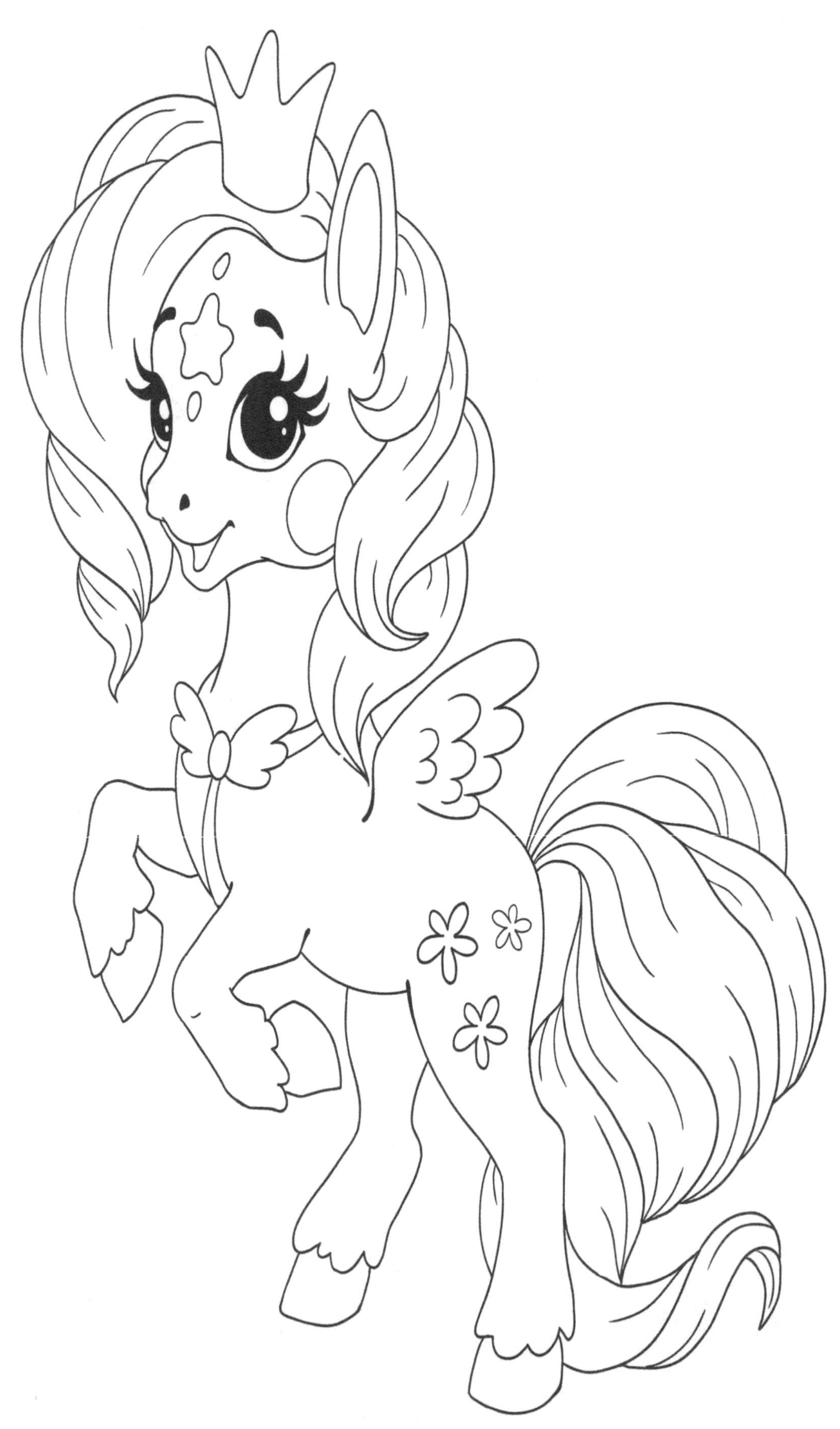

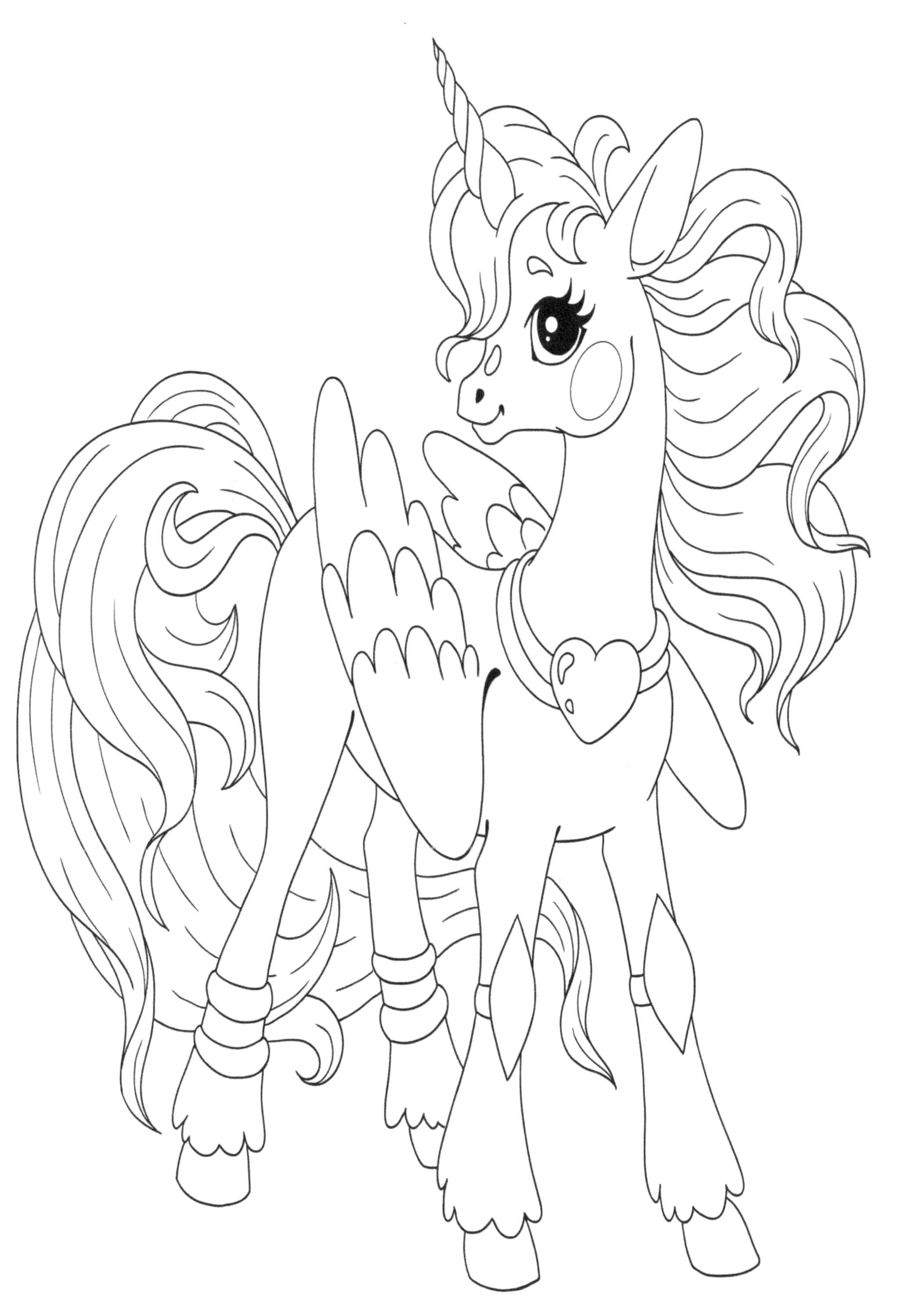

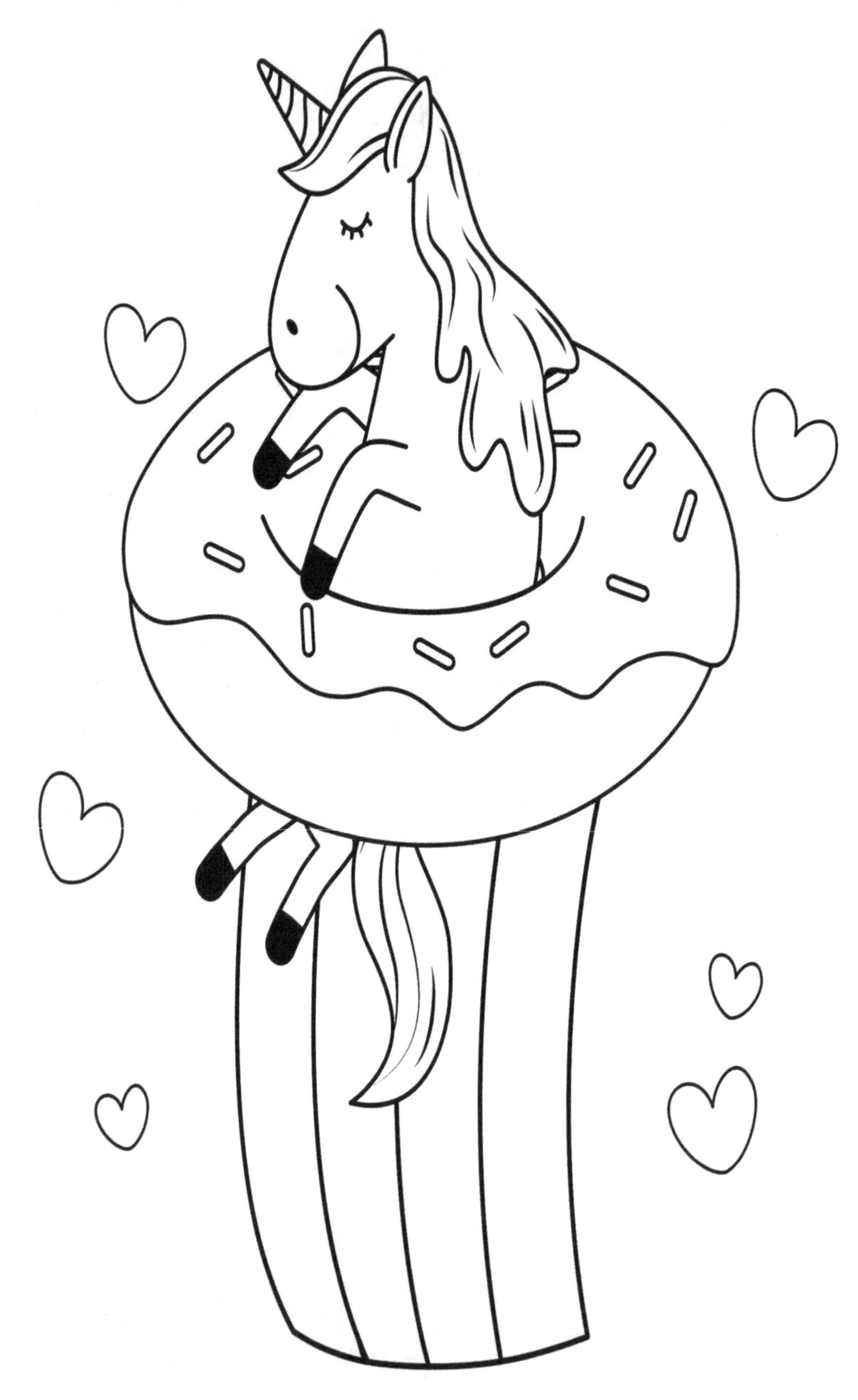

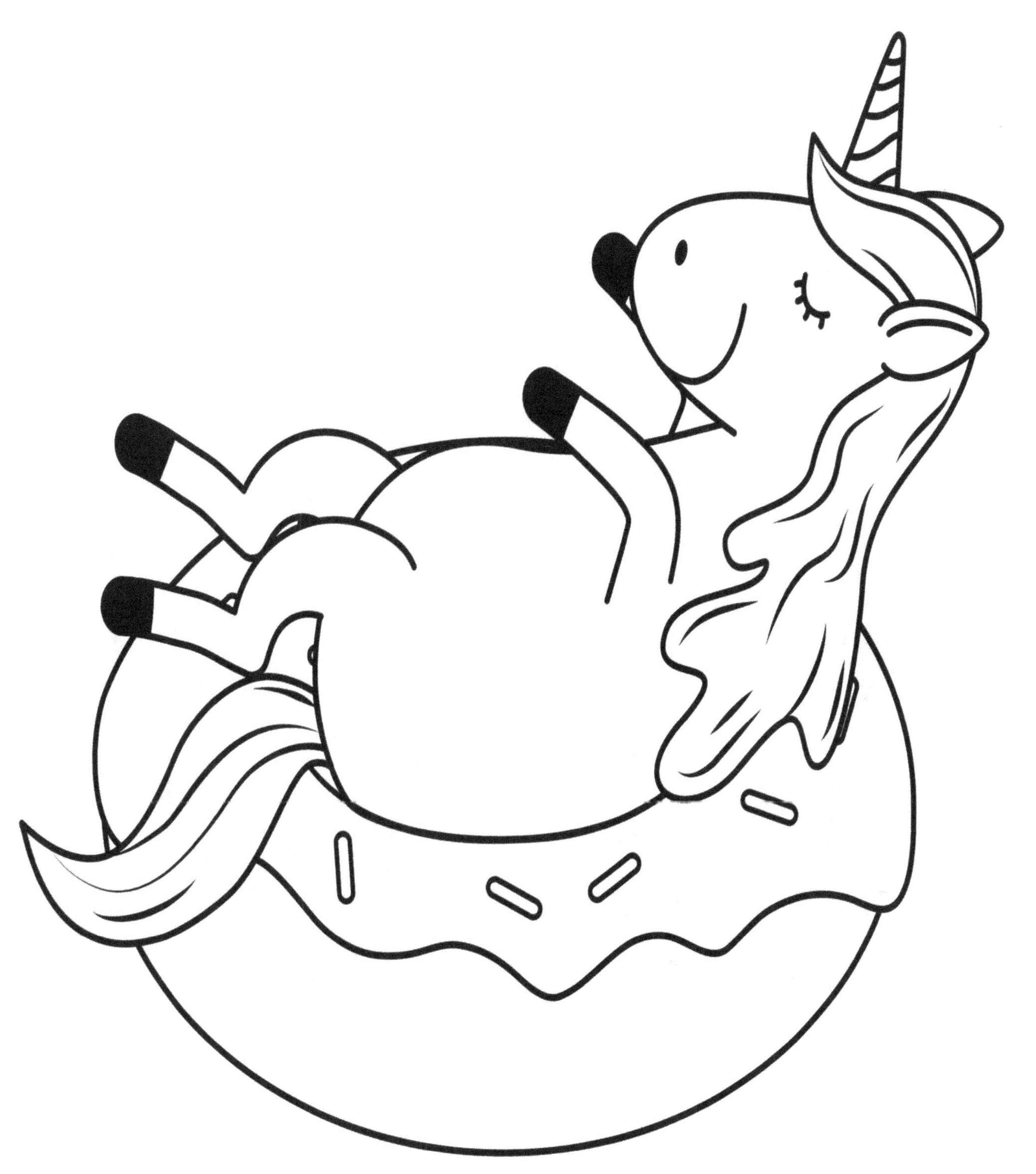

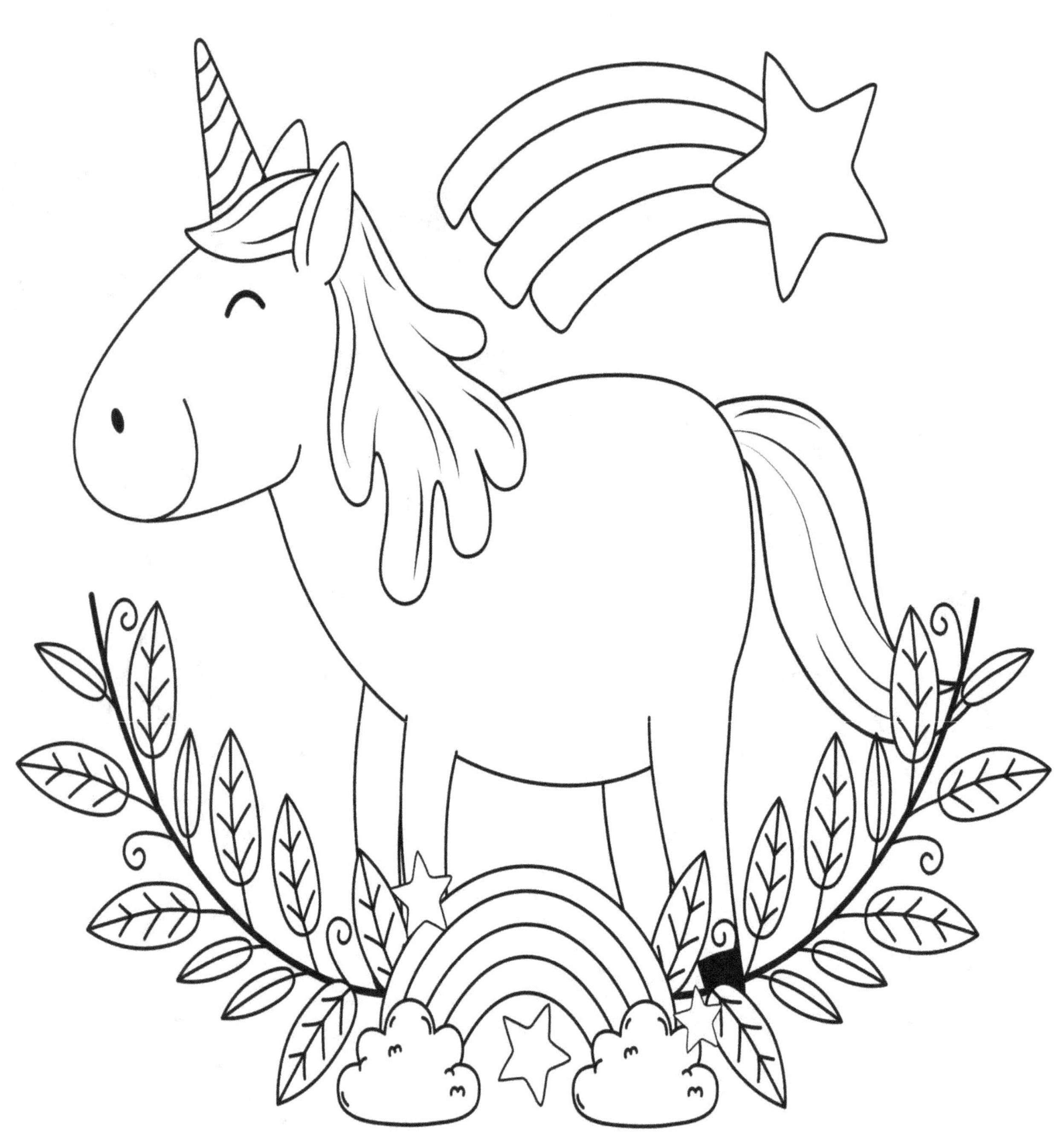

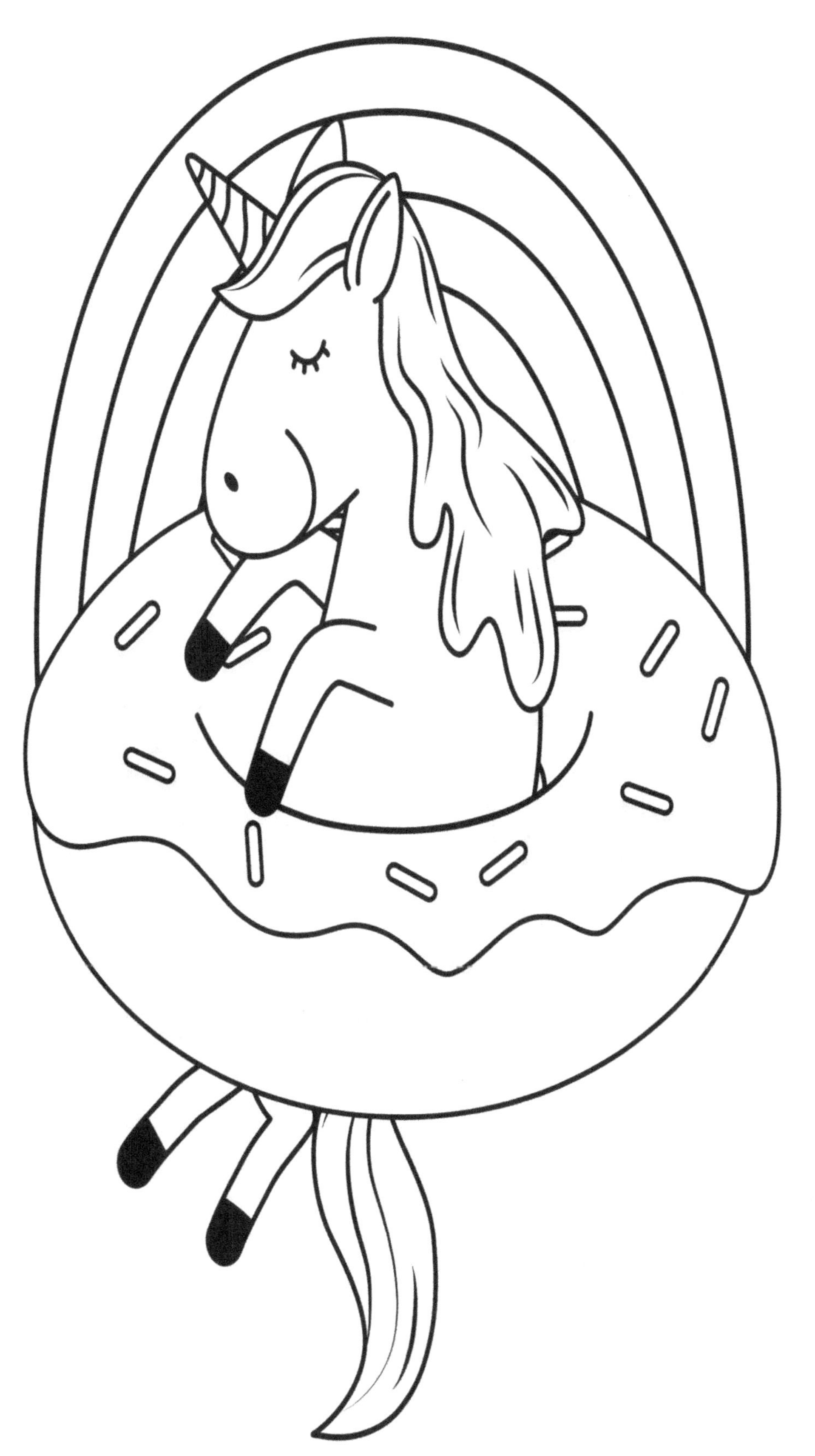

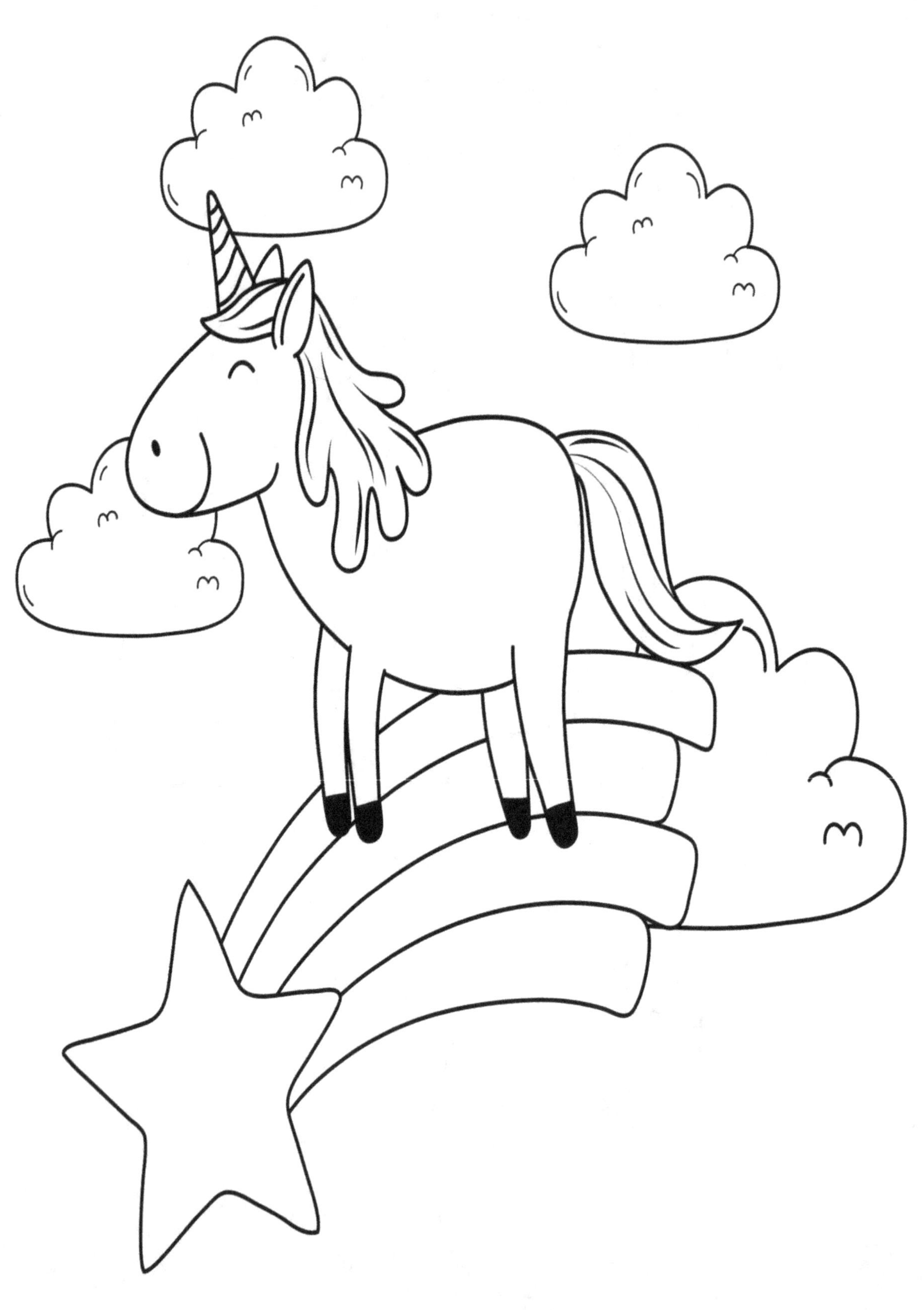

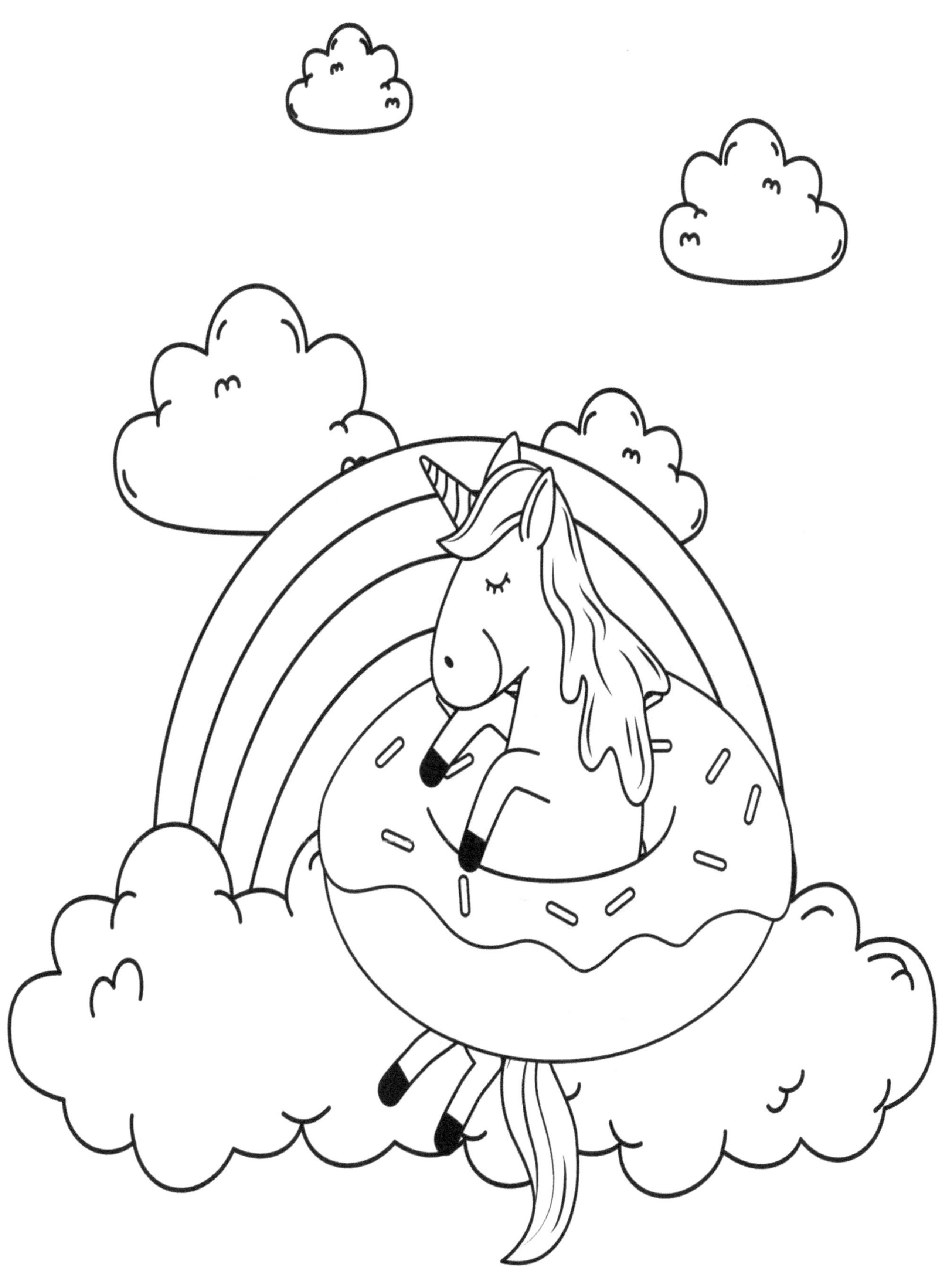

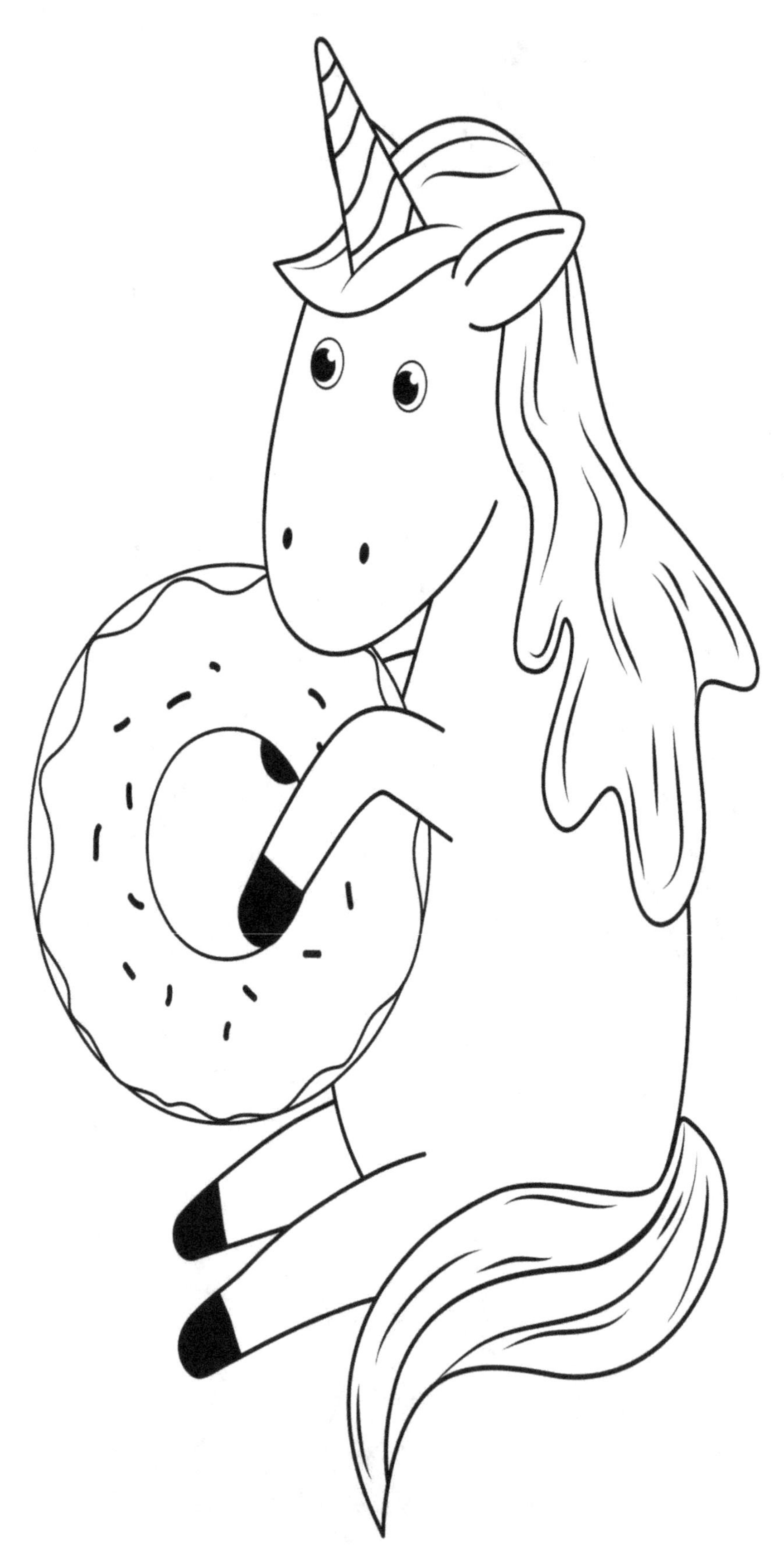

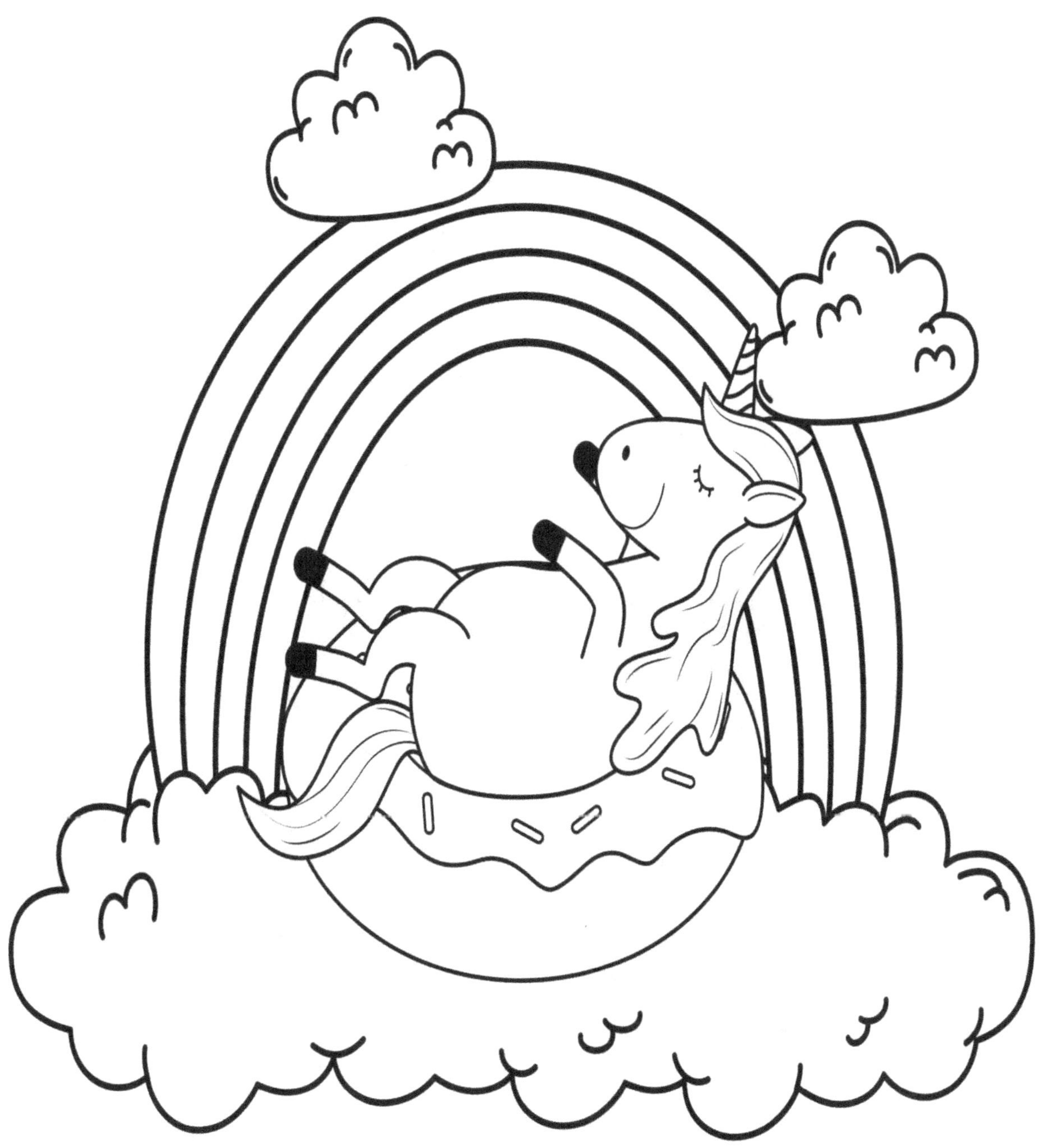

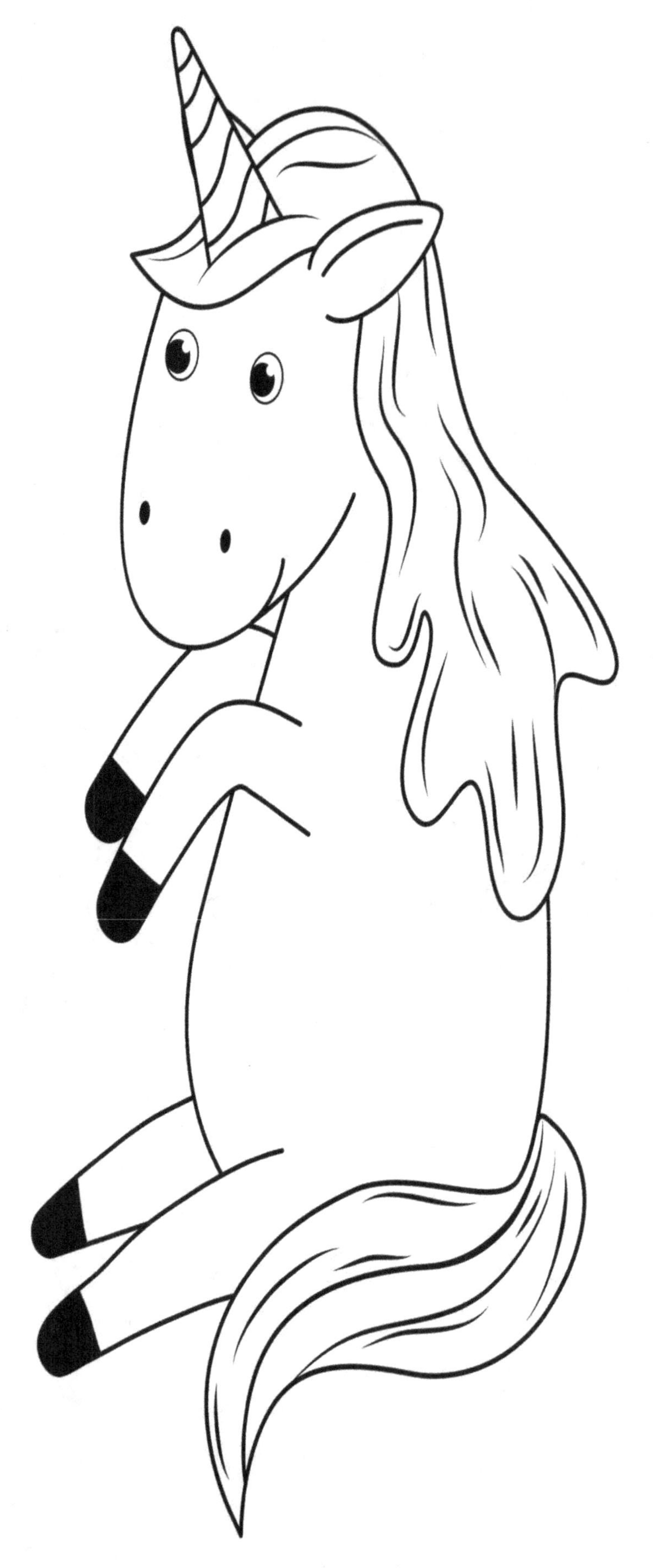

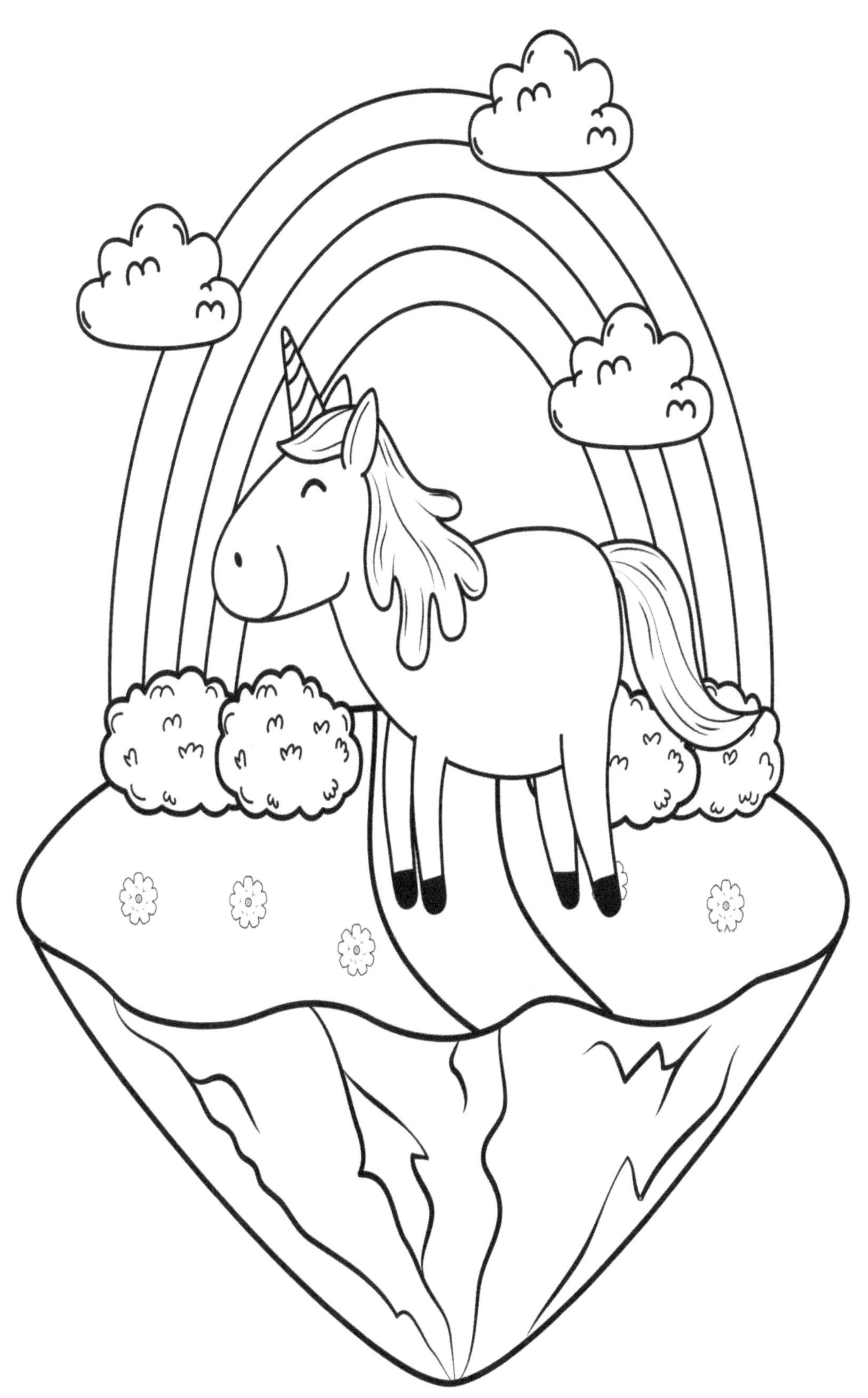

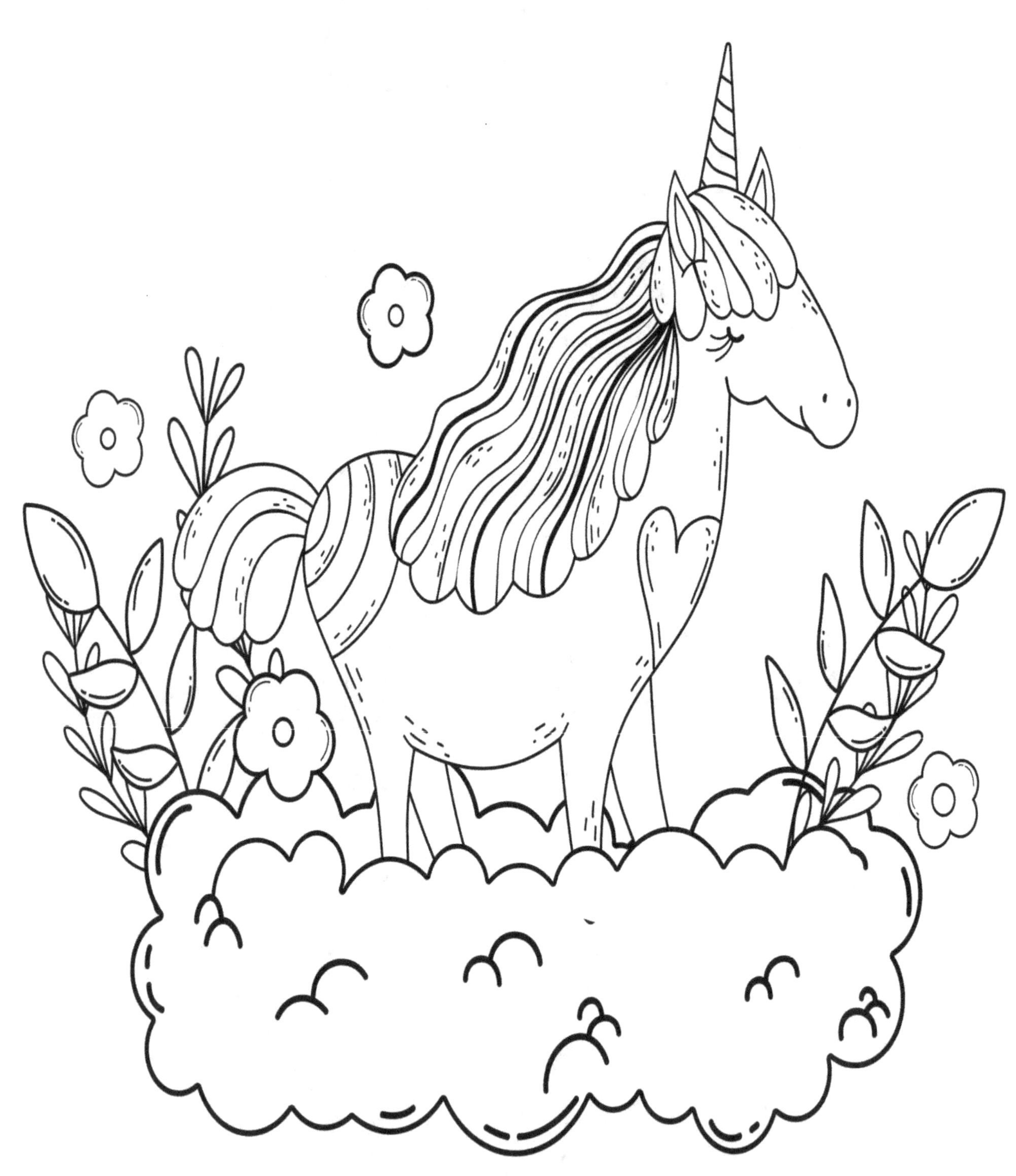

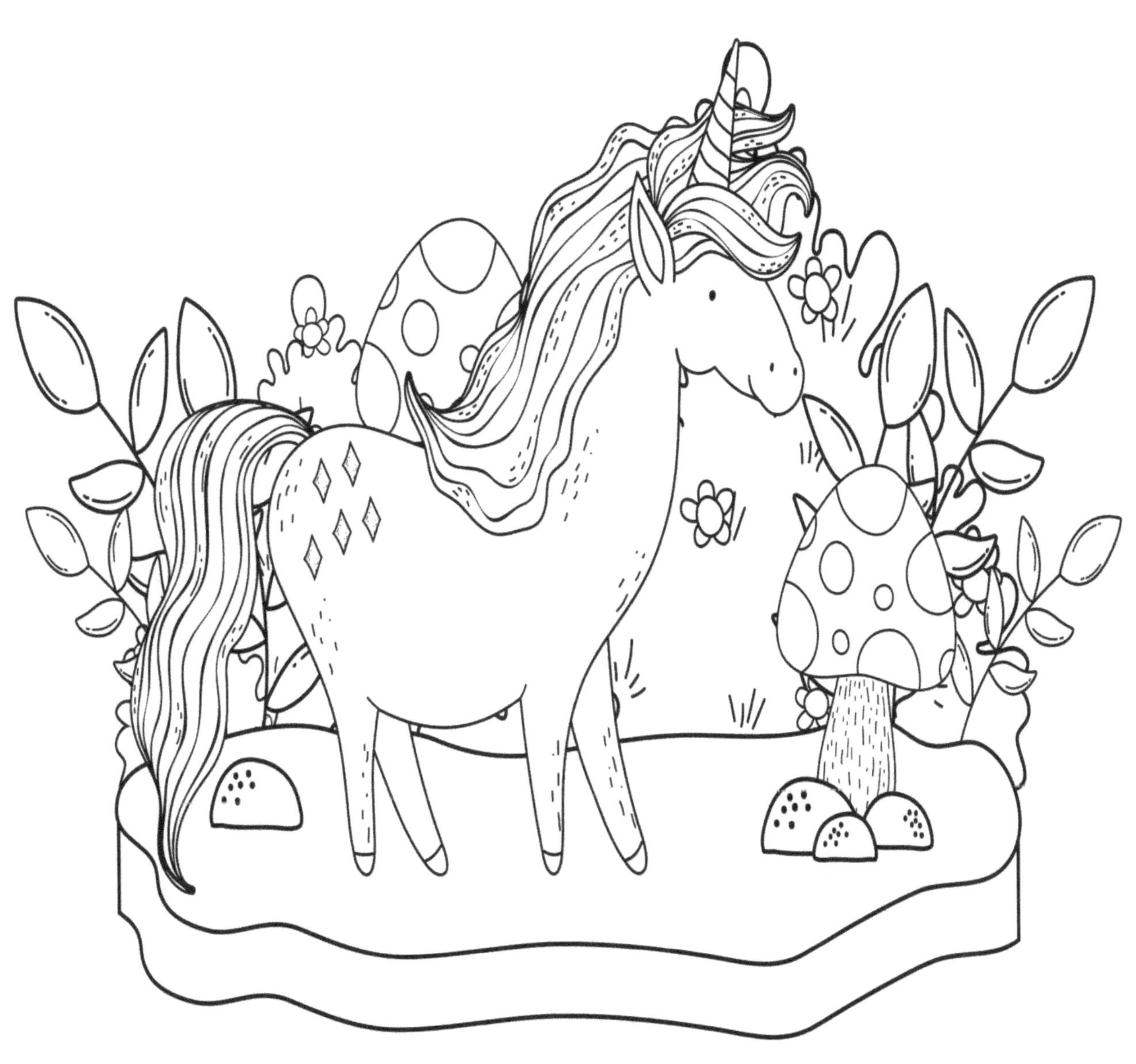

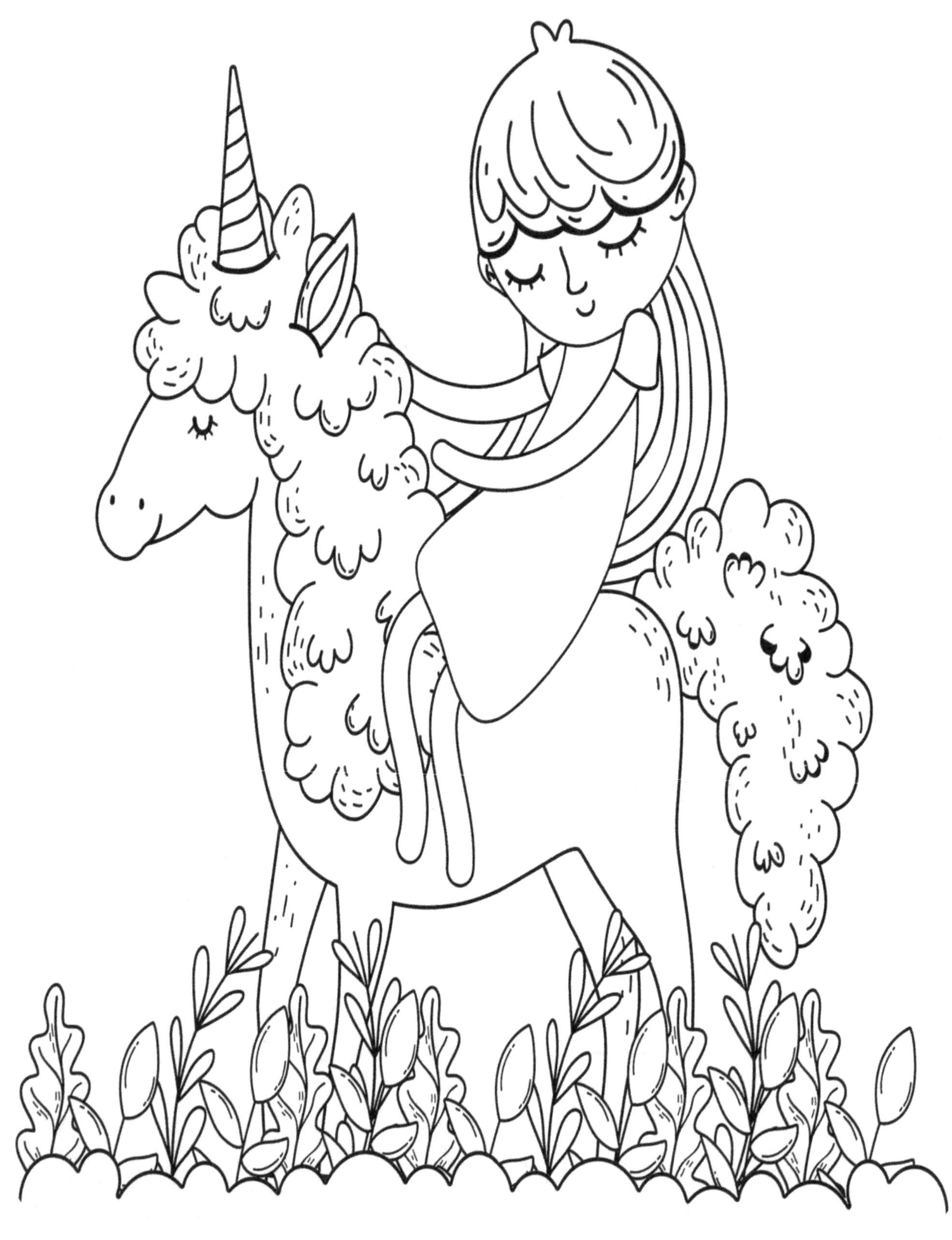

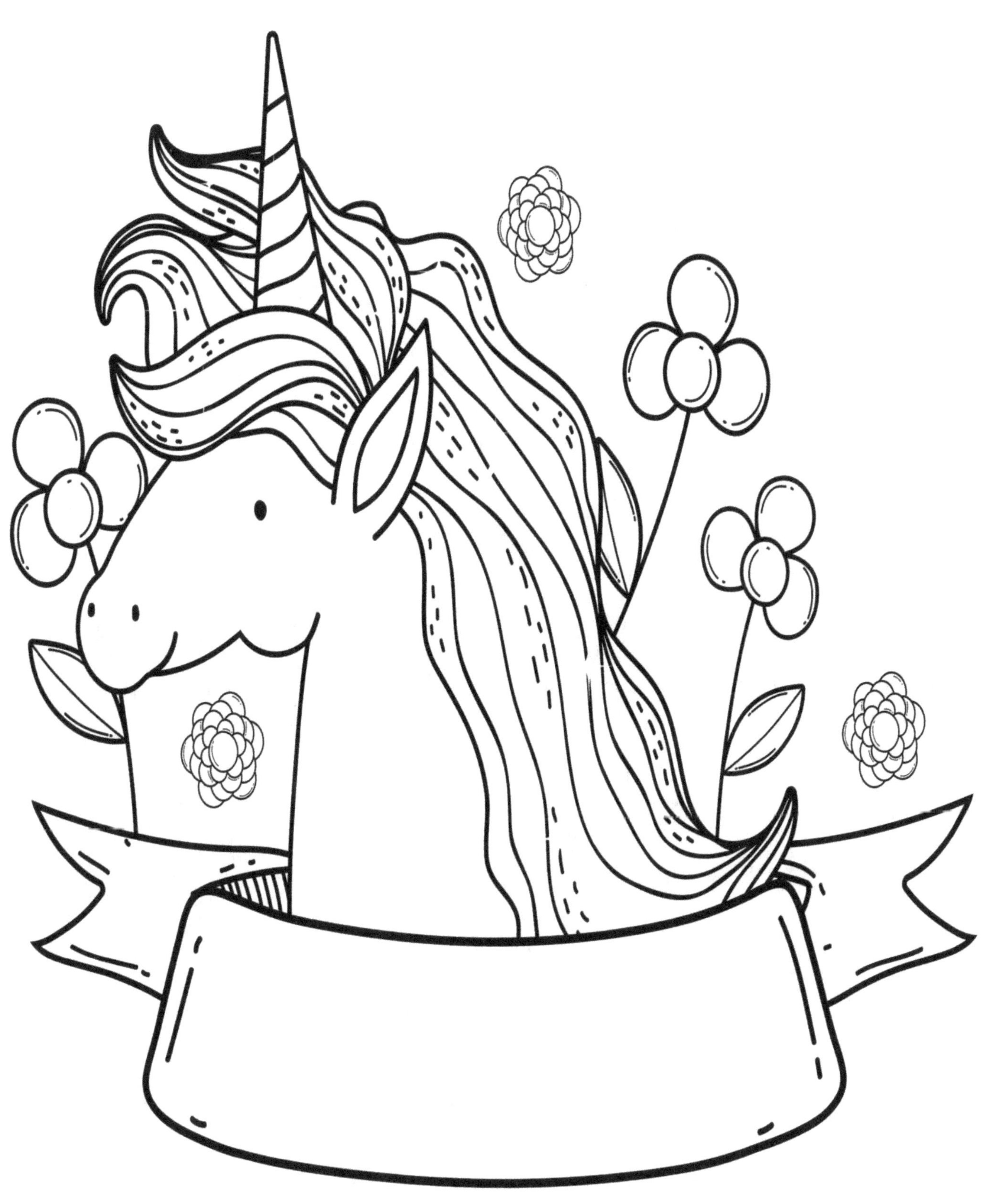

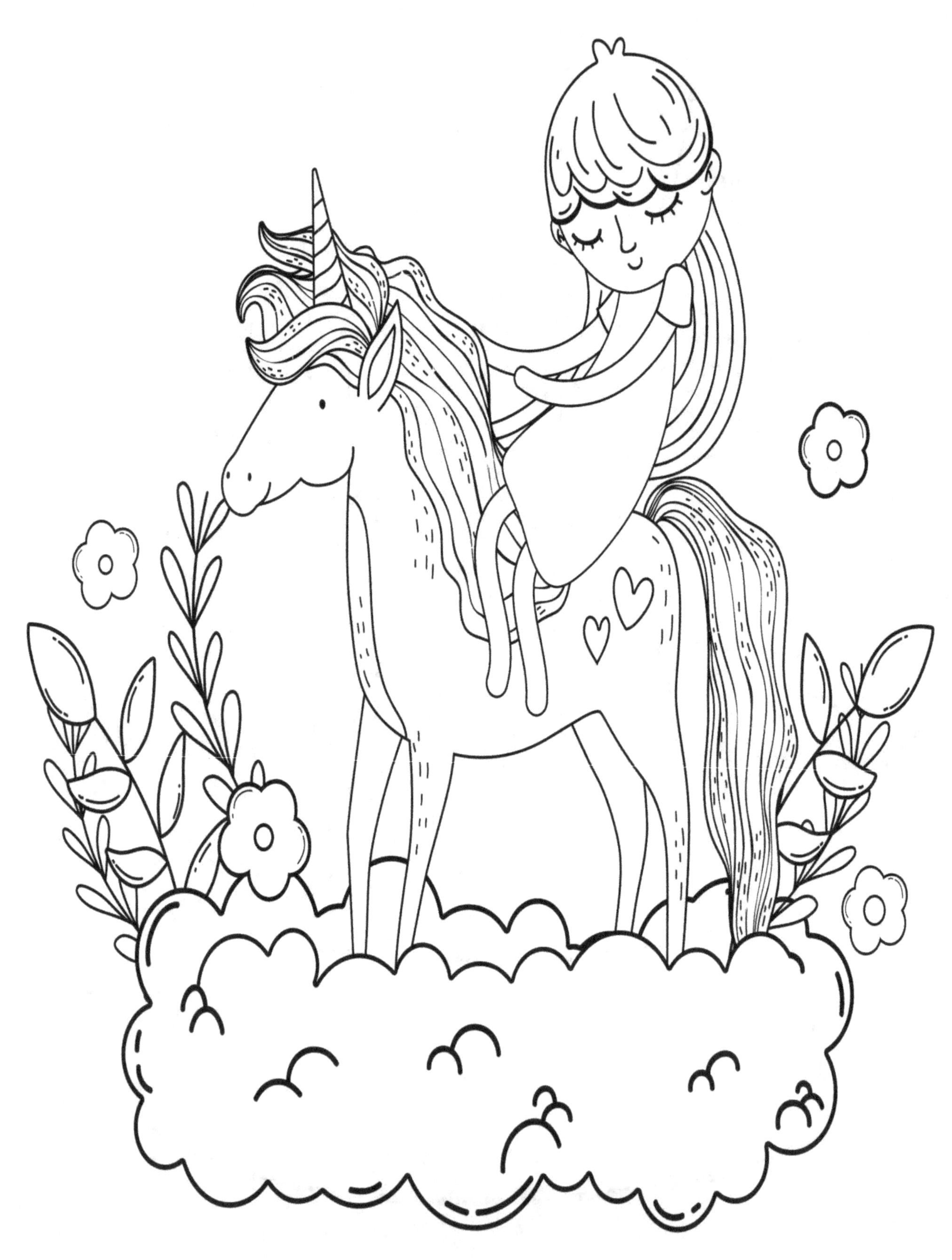